Mane Thoughts

Essays on Horsemanship

Tom Moates

Other Books by Tom Moates:

Discovering Natural Horsemanship
Round-Up: A Gathering of Equine Writings
Six Colts, Two Weeks, Volume I
Six Colts, Two Weeks, Volume II
Six Colts, Two Weeks, Volume III
Considering Horsemanship
The Christian Horseman's Companion
The Old Sleeper, A Spy Novel

The Honest Horsemanship Series:
A Horse's Thought
Between the Reins
Further Along the Trail
Going Somewhere
Passing It On

MANE THOUGHTS

ESSAYS ON HORSEMANSHIP

TOM MOATES

SPINNING SEVENS
PRESS

ISBN 978-0-9992465-6-6
Cover design by Tom Moates.
Front cover image (Niji) by Tom Moates.
Rear cover image (Jubal and Tom) by Teddy Carter.

Contents

Acknowledgements

As always, I must thank Harry Whitney for his tireless work to teach others what he has discovered to be true about getting better with horses—and that I have been able to learn so much from him. Self-professed king of "tired and grumpy," the truth is, Harry's sincere hope to convey helpful lessons to folks has endeared him to a couple of generations of humans hoping to improve their relationships with their horses, mules, and donkeys. I think there're even a few minis in there somewhere. So many thanks to you Harry.

A big thanks goes to the magazine editors who saw fit to publish some of these essays and allow me the opportunity to introduce some helpful horsemanship concepts to large readerships. In particular, I want to mention Emily Kitching at *Eclectic-Horseman* magazine and Holly Clanahan at the American Quarter Horse Association publications, *America's Horse* and *The American Quarter Horse Journal*. They allowed me quite a bit of elbow room to discuss horsemanship in ways not always found on the trail-more-traveled in the world of print.

A huge thanks to my horsemanship lesson clients and clinic attendees, for without y'all my scope of knowledge would be diminished and my ability to convey what I have learned about horsemanship most certainly would be considerably less than what it has become.

The photos in this book were taken by me except where otherwise noted in the captions. Many thanks to those whose pictures I am delighted to include to accompany these essays.

A special thanks to my wife Carol for putting up with my obsessive horse and writing endeavors. When it comes to those areas, I can be a bit, well, like some combination of a broken record and a thundering herd in a thunder storm.

I want to give my deepest gratitude to God for answering my prayers with blessings beyond my wildest dreams. To be able to work with horses every day and share what I discover on the page with readers is such a nourishment to my soul that it rather defies words.

And finally, it is you readers who make the books and articles possible by giving them an audience. I greatly appreciate all of the encouraging notes from you and for the ongoing support for these books that I dearly love to write.

INTRODUCTION

Horses and horsemanship. The pursuit to get better with horses drove me like a guy with his hair on fire seeks a water trough to find the best help I could over the past couple of decades. And I have been fortunate to find some great insights.

It is just my nature to strongly desire to share what I discover about horsemanship with others. Perhaps that's just a component of my other obsession, writing. Luckily, it was fairly early on in my quest to get better with horses that I was blessed to come across horsemanship clinician Harry Whitney.

I've covered aplenty about Harry in my other dozen published horse books, so I won't go into details on working with him here. Except to say that the essays compiled in this book span most of my horse years and that they were composed individually over time. Thus, I hope that quite a few brief introductions to Harry in these essays won't prove too redundant for the reader.

Also, the advancements I have made in horsemanship have come from picking things up from Harry, from teaching horsemanship to others, and of course from the school of horse knocks—but the underlying success of it all comes from getting horses to center their focus and from working with their minds. I sincerely hope that the variety of ways shown in these essays of how working with horses' thoughts can manifest and be implemented by humans will provide many interesting and productive opportunities for the aspiring horse person to grab an understanding of them.

Above all, I hope you can in some ways increase your fun

with these amazing equines by improving your relationships with them through some of the thoughts shared in these pages— and that reading this book will be both helpful and entertaining!

Tom Moates
Floyd, VA
July, 2022

Side-Pulls & Bits

Mirage sporting my Jamey Wilcox side-pull. (Photo: Olivia Wilkes)

Often, when a photo of me riding gets published and it is noticeable that the horse I'm on is wearing a side-pull rather than a bit and bridle, I get inquiries from folks. They want to know if that is indeed some kind of bitless headgear they see in the photo, just what is it, and why do I use it?

There are many varying opinions on the subject of bits and whether to use one or not. It certainly can be very confusing to consider just what is the best head gear to use for the horses in our care, especially for folks just starting out on their horsemanship journeys.

The answer in my case is that I ride in either a double jointed snaffle bit or my favorite side-pull—unless I am riding a client's horse who is already tacked up with whatever the client uses. Well, that's a bit of a fib to be honest, since I have not pulled out the snaffle in so long now that it is relegated to the bottom of the tack tub I carry in my horse-work-mobile. But, I would use it, no-worries, if I felt the urge, and I have no personal problem with folks using a bit. And I do make a point to have my own horses accustomed to the bit, as who knows what the future may bring and I want them all to get along in life with a minimum of hassle should someone at some point stick a bit in their mouths. However, the bit and bridle's second-class position in my tack bin does reveal my personal preference for the side-pull as my default choice, and I'll try to jot down a few thoughts on this here for the interested as I explore why that is.

Without getting really long winded—I'll cut to the chase and explain that there are two main considerations that guided me to the point of where I am today regarding my head-gear preference. One is an understanding of the use of the reins and the other is having sat-in many times on horsemanship clinician Harry Whitney's "horse skull discussion."

As is likely the case with any uninitiated horseperson, when

I started out with horses I had no idea about what bit to use. I knew that one should use a bit because I had seen plenty of westerns and that's what people do, right? They bit a horse. As I began to sift through the opinions on bits, I came across all kinds of chatter. Before long, however, I began to notice that most people that I came across directed their thinking about the bit as a means of "controlling" the horse. If a horse "misbehaved," for example, try a different bit and get one that does the job of keeping the horse in-line.

Central to my concerns from the beginning were the horses' best interests and causing them minimal agony as I tried to learn how to work those reins effectively. And so, I began to worry about making sure that the bit I used wasn't going to cause a horse pain or grief as I worked to get my novice hands more refined with the reins. However, as time went on and I observed folks riding, it wasn't the bits that stood out so much to me as it was seeing some startling differences in how various people handled the reins. The results their hands produced on horses was profound.

Eventually, at that early stage, I settled on a single jointed snaffle bit. I am sure I arrived at that conclusion after plenty of reading, watching videos, and talking to some local horse folks that got me picking up on the natural horsemanship movement that was well underway at the time, since that bit was advocated by many in that realm.

The first snaffle bit I got, interestingly, was completely flattened on one side by my wife's horse Niji...thanks to whatever training the gelding had encountered earlier in life. He had such anxiety and a busy mouth that he literally flattened a metal bit! I've never seen one so altered by teeth before or since. I keep that one hanging in my office to remind me how much difference our horsemanship can make in the lives of horses

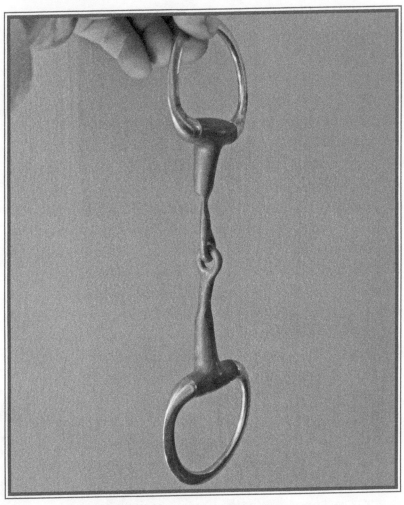

The snaffle bit that was flattened by Niji.

because over time I was able to work with Niji to the point that his mouth became perfectly still when we'd go riding.

The key to this change in Niji is the key to using the reins in a way to best reduce tension in a horse—that is to make sure that each time a rein is engaged that the horse's thought follows along with our feel on the rein. Said another way, the reins are used for communication (they transfer the feel we present) and are not a mechanical device intended to physically manipulate the horses by pulling. They are best activated by the hands and not the biceps.

Each time we pick up a rein and offer for the horse to think in a direction, we do well to see that the horse lets go of other thoughts, follows along with what we present, and takes a good interest in the direction we ask for. Then we release, and so we hope to build the horse's understanding and confidence in what those reins mean, and we hope to eliminate resistance to the reins in the horse. Whole volumes can be written on this subject, but for now I'll just say that when I began to use the reins consistently in this way with Niji, he got better at letting go of other things on his mind when I engaged a rein and he became much more willing to think along (and thus go along) with what I asked.

And this gets us to one half of the explanation of my present preference for the side-pull. If one truly gets a horse following a feel presented on the reins, then that communication is going to look pretty much the same on a side-pull as it would with a snaffle bit. It is the understanding and usage of the reins that really makes the difference. And getting the job done well without gear in the horse's mouth appeals to me.

As an aside, I have worked with horses that have had such negative experiences with bits that simply putting a bit in their mouths brought up huge anxiety that was in itself a blockage to a better relationship with the human when riding. I started carrying my side-pull when going to work clients' horses in part because of this fact. On several occasions I have been able to get down to the work of improving the understanding of the reins more easily without the extra, established negative cue of having a bit in the horse's mouth, and then work my way back to the bit.

I should take a second here and say that by side-pull I am

talking about head gear for the horse that looks much like a halter with reins that attach to either side. In fact, one can use a halter for this by attaching reins, but the proper side-pulls I am acquainted with have at least one additional strap going underneath the horse's jaw that helps to keep the head gear in place and especially helps to prevent the side-pull from getting catawampus and pulling the rings where the reins connect up into the horse's eyes.

To answer another often asked question, the side-pull I use is a leather model made by Jamey Wilcox who owns SJ Saddlery in Rogersville, TN [www.sjsaddleryinc.com]. There are many kinds of side-pulls available from a variety of vendors.

A side-pull always has the right rein attached to the right side and the left rein attached to the left side. This arrangement is thus quite directional in usage and allows for excellent releases (when the rider releases his ask on the reins they immediately provide slack), and should not be confused with other head gear that has the reins crossing under the horse's jaw. Also, the side-pull is not a hackamore, which has the main feature of a nose band where the reins both attach to a central knot located underneath the horse's chin.

Even before I had a clear vision of using a side-pull for riding more finished horses, I already would ride young horses I was starting in just a halter. One of the reasons for that also contributes to my liking the side-pull. The first rides I put on young horses typically are in the rope halter I have been using for ground work—first just with the lead rope to one side, and then soon with the loose end of the lead rope tied back around to the halter like reins. Then, when I introduce a snaffle bit, I often ride with both the halter and the bridle. In this way I can let go of the reins on the bit and pick up the lead rope "reins" on the halter if the horse gets a strong thought and goes to pulling

Harry Whitney giving the "horse skull talk" in the bunk house at his place in Salome, Arizona. (Photo: Harry Whitney Horsemanship)

so that I do not "get in the horse's mouth" right away and begin a trip down the road of negative bit experiences that can cause discomfort and resistance to the bit. In the same way, I find it sometimes good to have a side-pull on a horse when teaching less experienced people to ride as it is less rude to the horse if the students don't have a good sense of feel for the reins and get a little strong handed.

My second reason for gravitating towards the side-pull by default these days is witnessing Harry Whitney's "horse skull talk." If you have never seen a horse's skull up close, it is well worth the time to investigate. There are some amazing things to be noticed, like how those long bony ends of the jaw on each side go clear up behind the eyes and through the skull and are visible at the top of the head in dimples you can see moving when a horse chews—who knew? Another notable point that Harry shows and allows participants to feel for ourselves, is just

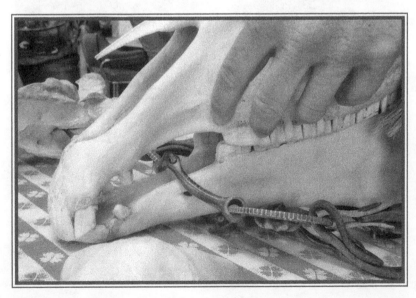

Harry demonstrates how different bits work in relation to the horse's bone structure in the mouth. (Photo: Harry Whitney Horsemanship)

how sharp the upper surface of the two long bones on the lower jaw are where the bit rests. It is plain to see and feel just how painful leveraging a bit against a scant bit of flesh and those sharp edged bones can be. Seeing that really impressed on me why horses can get bracey with the bit...that has got to hurt! And when pain is inflicted, how can you facilitate relaxation and positive connections with a horse?

Harry will take a few different bits and show how they work in the horse's mouth with the skull as a prop. A leverage bit with a chin strap, whether long shanked or short, clearly is designed so that the reins cause the bit to clamp down against that bottom jaw bone in the mouth, and with leverage that means the pressure is amplified many times beyond what the hand itself is offering. I've never forgotten that visual from the first time I saw the mechanics of it on the skull; it was profound.

When I first saw the skull talk, I was riding in a single joint egg butt snaffle bit. It was during that talk that I saw that even an egg butt with it's elongated oval rings can have some leverage effect on the bit, and I vowed to get a ring snaffle—the reins slide readily in a round ring and aren't able to produce any leverage. And Harry also pointed out another issue that can arise with a single jointed snaffle bit that caused me to go to a double jointed snaffle. The single jointed snaffle can bunch up and cause the joint of the bit to create an inverted V, poking upwards, and thus potentially poke the soft tissue in the top of the horse's mouth. The double jointed snaffle really can't bunch up in the same way. And even if it did to some extent, the center link is a flat bar that would press against the tissues in the top of the mouth rather than the more poky and higher rising single point of a single joint.

The side-pull avoids all of these potentially painful pitfalls, which no-doubt weighs on my decision to grab the side-pull by default, even though I am at ease with the thought of using the double jointed snaffle. I always enjoy seeing how good and consistent I can get the reins working with a horse. I delight in seeing a horse become very light in the hand with the side-pull because I marvel at how good that can get in comparison to a bit, which one would think is a more sensitive means of transferring feel as the mouth of a horse is magnificently delicate.

It boils down to the fact that if my horsemanship and my hands are skilled enough, and my focus is on the task as it should be, then the side-pull is as good as the snaffle, and I find that rewarding to get working. As a teacher riding in clinics and lessons (and as shows up in photos in articles) with the side-pull with excellent results, it also helps to debunk some of the assumptions and straight-up myths about bits and their usage. It shows a bit isn't necessary to "control" a horse. Plus, it is both fun for me and, I think, doing horses a service to challenge many of the mainstream suppositions about bits.

Reins

Mirage and me. (Photo: Olivia Wilkes)

The reins—those thin strips of matter that connect human hands to a horse's head—are a hugely important bit of tack. And yet, it isn't the reins themselves or even the particular headgear they attach to that really matters. Regarding this, it is how a person uses the reins that produces the most profound effect on how horses go about business with a rider. A horse's reactions to the reins also can be a barometer revealing the nature of the relationship between them and us.

Simply stated, I've come to understand that there are two approaches to using reins. One is a mechanical approach. This is where a rider has it in mind that the reins are used to move a horse's body around, an arrangement something akin to using a steering wheel on a car. The other is when the reins are understood to be conduits for communication between the rider and the horse, and vice versa. In this scenario, the reins are more like telephone wires (remember those?) allowing the rider and horse to speak to one another; the rider makes a light suggestion and it is left up to the horse to agree to move himself around willingly. These two approaches produce two very different feels and results in a horse.

Many folks are familiar with the old equine adage and methodology, "Kick to go, pull to stop, pull the left rein to go left, and the right rein to go right." Simple, right? That is a very mechanical understanding of how to ride a horse and use the reins for steering and stopping. If the horse was a machine like a motorcycle, that would be just fine. The problem with this approach when considering the horse is that it only addresses moving a horse's body around. There need be no consideration for how the horse feels about the situation or even that the rider pay attention to feedback from the horse.

"Every time you pick up a rein," I've heard my mentor, horsemanship clinician Harry Whitney, say many times, "wait for the horse's thought to come through before you release.... *How many* times is that? *Every* time!"

Harry's quote is the perfect means to begin this discussion on how and why to use the reins for communication rather that just as a steering mechanism. Horses learn from the releases we offer them. If we want to back a horse during some ground work, for example, we offer a feel on the lead rope (perhaps a slight wiggle) and then when the horse tries a backwards step, we release the ask and offer a sweet spot between us. Build on this and soon it can take very little feel on the lead rope to get that horse backing willingly. The horse desires to be in balance with us and will get in the habit of hunting up the sweet spot we offer if we are consistent with how we handle asks and releases. It is no different with handling the reins. Let's look at an example of the kind of reactions typical of mechanical rein handling.

It is pretty common to see a horse tense up when a rider touches the reins. For instance, say we see a rider sitting on a horse and the reins are laying on the horse's neck. The rider decides it is time to go somewhere and he picks up the reins. The horse's immediate reaction is to bring his head up, tense, push his nose out, and brace against the bit (or side-pull, hackamore, etc.). These observable clues provide insight into how the horse feels about the person engaging the reins in this example—it is an ill feeling, and the horse readily displays resistance against the feel on the reins even before the rider has asked anything of the horse.

Then, perhaps the rider engages the right rein to go to the right. The horse steps to the right, but we notice that his head is actually tilted in the opposite direction on the end of his neck and his eyes even look hard back to the left. This is a pretty good indication that the horse is not feeling good about what is being asked and is not a willing partner in getting the job done of going to the right. He is going to the right, perhaps even immediately, but it is an automatic reaction to the right rein and not a thoughtful one. It is likely that the tension will have him turning to the right braced like a board. A horse in this scenario may even be conceding to the right rein to avoid a painful confrontation with a bit, so it actually is an act of avoidance rather

I begin engaging the right rein (simply a lead rope tied back to a rope halter) to ask Mirage to think to the right. (Photo: Carol Moates)

Mirage, hearing my request, begins turning her head and looking in the direction I'm indicating with the rein. (Photo: Carol Moates)

Mirage has thought along with the right rein and now commits to bending and stepping to the right. (Photo: Carol Moates)

than willingness. The horse certainly associates this predicament with the rider, understanding full well that the rider is doing it to him.

So, if a rider is getting a quick right turn with a horse, what difference does it make if the horse is relaxed and willing? Well, to some it may not matter a lick. The job gets done quickly, the horse didn't buck the rider off..so what's all the fuss?

The above example represents what I think of as a mechanical use of the reins. The fuss is that it is very likely unhelpful in building the kind of relationship we want to have with our horses if we are interested in acquiring a deeper willingness from our horses. With greater willingness comes a level of performance that can not be achieved in a mechanical way. It will not be because—as with humans—a horse who is not feeling his best will not perform his best. When a rider achieves a higher level of togetherness and willingness from a horse, the horse is thoughtfully focused on the task at hand, participating in it with the rider, rather than mentally avoiding it. That smoothness of relationship reduces tension in the horse because he is focused with us.

So, back to Harry's quote and getting to a horse's thoughts. Loose in their own worlds, horses almost always have their eyes on their primary thoughts. Observe a herd of horses out in an open place and notice that when they get moving towards something they nearly always are looking at it. If we engage the right rein but the horse is looking back hard to the left, what does that say about where his primary thought is? It's certainly not with us. And horses don't come into the world wanting to think opposite what a person offers. The truth is that we train this resistance and opposition to the reins into them by not paying attention to where they are thinking when we offer releases.

When Harry says to "wait for the horse's thought to come through before you release the rein," he is talking about getting the horse literally thinking along with what we offer as part of the function of the reins. Always, always, and double especially always at first when establishing meaning in the reins with a horse, wait for the thought to come through in a direction offered by a rein before releasing the rein.

What does it look like for a horse to think in the direction of a rein? The person should look for such clues as the horse looking in the direction offered by the rein, a lowering of the head, a softening of the pole and neck muscles, a bend in the neck and through the body in the direction of the rein, and a general sense of interest in the horse to go that way.

If we follow Harry's thinking, we can set up another example that may be helpful in understanding this concept of using the reins. Say a rider is riding along and decides to go through an open gate to the left. She engages the left rein. The horse steps around to the left, stiff as a board and looking hard back hard to the right. That's not the kind of reaction our rider wants in her horse to the rein. But now the horse is facing the open gate right where the rider has the mind to go.

In the mechanical rein world, that just worked out brilliantly. Release the rein and through the gate she goes lickity-split. But in the world of true rein communication between rider and horse, that is not okay. Per Harry's advice, even though the rider wants to go through the gate and is now pointed right at the gate, she must not release the rein because the horse is not yet thinking to the left. So, she holds onto the left rein and keeps her horse circling to the left, looking and feeling for signs that the horse is finally thinking to the left. Finally, the horse's head lowers, she sees those dark brown eyes give a good look to the left, and she releases.

Perfect timing! Only now, they are going away from the gate in the opposite direction than what the rider intended. But, so what? What is more important, to have your horse go through a gate or to have a horse who is soft, willing, and has no tension or resistance when you engage a rein?

Our rider may need to drop her other ambitions and

Mekenna takes a nice look to the right as I softly engage the right rein as we go along. Owned by my brother Ken and his wife Melissa, she is a half sister to Mirage. We are riding at their place in Georgia. (Photo: Melissa Moates)

spend some time working on this right there. And it might be a little while before her horse gets mentally with her on those reins and also is lined up to go through the gate. This is one of the dilemmas of horsemanship—often the quickest answer isn't the one that brings about willingness and relaxation in a horse. Thus it takes time, effort, and understanding to set things up to have a horse truly with a person. But once established, what a great feeling and what wonderful and lasting performance can be achieved with a horse.

There is a vast depth to the aspects of using the reins that can be addressed, but none of that counts for much if your horse is not thinking along with the reins in the first place. Without the reins attaching directly to the horse's mind, any endeavor with the reins will be some kind of mechanical exercise.

Spend a little extra time at first setting things up so that when you barely touch a rein your horse is looking where you'd like to go, bending softly through his body, and really taking you there willingly and then enjoy that togetherness for the rest of your horse's days. Having the reins working well and using them to help a horse to relax and be willing partner can be the key that unlocks so many other things we desire to do well with our horses, too. Whether it be picking up and setting a horse's foot exactly where you want it on a narrow trail, getting a sweet half-halt, turning instantly to cut off a cow, or even a performing a piaffe, getting true communication working with your horse through the reins is the place to start. It likely will be one of the best investments of time you ever make, and your horse will thank you for it with many miles of partnership and good feelings between you.

Those Spots

Now there's a horse with some spots! Stoney was my wife Carol's horse, and while those aren't the kind of spots I'm talking about in this essay, he is magnificent to behold. (Photo: Carol Moates)

It is pretty common for horse people to refer to problem areas in horses as "spots." One spot that crops up often, for example, when doing a little groundwork is, if a person walks quickly towards a horse, the horse may become tense or even shy away. Another spot can be a horse who is grumpy about having the girth tightened up. There are a bunch of spots that can crop up in horses—problem areas that when not tended to at best remain little nagging barriers between humans and horses, and at worst become flash points to set off big explosions that we never want to see in our horses.

Along the trail of my horsemanship journey, it has become rather instinctive for me to search out these spots just in the regular course of working with horses. Horsemanship clinician Harry Whitney was the first horseman I saw who made it an ongoing, active mission to find and clear out these kinds of spots in horses. After spending some time with Harry, my primary focus became working to improve how horses feel about doing things with me rather that just getting horses to do those things. As a result, I became increasingly aware of finding these spots and working to clear them out.

So, what does it look like to recognize and work on horse spots?

Let's take the first example from above as an illustration. I tend to approach horses matter-of-factly...sort of carelessly. If there is apprehension in the horse, I sometimes intentionally fumble about with the lead rope balled up in my hands in the air sort of between my face and the horse's face as I approach. This may get a horse quite nervous. Sometimes a horse even may fling her head in the air and back away.

But, such an approach by a person need not worry a horse. If a horse is confident in the presence of a person, even a dreadfully careless approach shouldn't bother the horse if the person has no ill intent. Also, it is important to realize that this undesirable reaction can come about if a horse is not wanting to focus on the human but is thinking about something else. Then the human's actions that require some of her attention may be what is causing the tension. In other words, a horse can be fine with my spastic approach if she is focused on me but the same horse can be quite bothered if my approach is interrupting a though that she has elsewhere that she feels she needs to pay attention to.

When helping a horse along in training, this trouble spot can be seen very early on and I work to clear it out so that it does not remain to worry the horse moving forward. Clearing it out means that I will approach the horse carelessly, fumbling with the lead rope, and keep up the shenanigans until some relaxation comes into the horse, and then quit. If the horse's head shoots up as I move towards her, for instance, then I just keep approaching until the head drops and the worry fades.

Often a horse shows huge relief when contact is finally made and I touch her with my hands and the balled up lead rope. That relief is evident in the head dropping, sometimes some licking and chewing starts up, and the whole horse visibly lets down as the situation is understood to be okay and not requiring high alert. Then, I repeat this scenario. Over some time—often after only a few repeats—increasing relaxation should result if my timing and feel of presentation are correct.

The second example mentioned at the start was cinching up a horse. Rather than just tightening a cinch, it is a good practice to notice and sense how the horse is reacting and feeling about being cinched. If there is a spot there where the horse gets pinched up about the cinching, I'm getting in there and poking around (often literally with my thumb or the handle of a flag) to see if the horse can let some of that anxiety go. Poking a horse can bring up the tension at first, and sometimes the whole horse twitches with each poke. But soon, that equine earthquake begins to be less reactive. I quit the poking or move to other spots when the horse begins to loosen up and relax to reinforce that releasing tension is the right choice. Eventually, horses can really enjoy the poking in this formerly tight and guarded area, and the activity feels more like giving them a massage than creating an aggravation.

Another good example of a spot is that when leading or circling a horse, sometimes the lead rope can worry a horse. I may toss the lead rope across a horse's back as we walk along. Sometimes that can bring about a pretty big worried reaction. It may be helpful to pause with whatever else was going on and work on that rope anxiety and clear it out to avoid it keeping the relationship from being as good as it might otherwise be.

I reach out with the loose end of the lead rope in my left hand and touch my horse Festus with it to see if there's a spot of concern as he trots a circle around me. (Photo: Carol Moates)

The thing about these little things is that they are the same as the big things—it is just the time and place where we notice them that makes them little or big. Catching them little is way better than hoping we survive them when they have been overlooked and they show up in a big way when we are riding on the trail or trying to get a horse into a trailer.

Some years ago, I was hired to restart a very tall, very athletic off-the-track Thoroughbred. This horse resembled a kite on a string in a hurricane when he arrived to his new home. Over time, things began to settle down and the horse came around in many nice ways with some work, both in the ground-work and with riding him. Still, I poked around in some areas that people often don't think to address, keeping an awareness for any spots that might show up. One was playing with a lariat all over the horse: around the barrel, up and down the legs, and so on.

Things mellowed out pretty well after a couple of rather exciting early sessions. I was thinking that we were wrapping up that hind-end-with-the-rope deal. But then, I happened to play with the rope high on the hind quarters and got it up under his tail for the first time. Oh my...now there was a spot! A very specific spot. The horse had a BIG reaction about that spot with the rope, and he charged forward and took tremendous offence.

I worked quite a bit off-and-on over a few sessions get-ting the rope under his tail until he was okay with it: approach-ing getting the rope under there; he'd clamp his tail and scoot forward; I'd hang in there until he relaxed some; then released by letting the rope drop down; then bringing it a bit further up under the tail, and so on. Finally, he became perfectly okay with it. At first he had clamped his tail so hard that it held the rope in the very spot that worried him and off he'd go. Eventually, it got so good that working a rope around under his tail actually cued him to relax his tail and there would be no clamping at all. The horse learned that he had the power to get rid of the rope from under his tail by relaxing his tail.

*I work on getting my horse Jubal okay with the rope up under his tail.
(Photo: Carol Moates)*

"Great!" I thought. "He's never going to be used to rope a steer and get hung up with a rope under his tail and kill somebody, anyway, but at least that's one more area where this horse has reduced anxiety. And with this big fella, we need all of that we can get!"

Fast forward a few sessions. We were in the round pen and I was trying to get this horse to transition from the trot to the lope without losing his mind and blasting around. He was really struggling with it. During one attempt to ask him to think forward and canter, he blew big-time. He blew so hard that he ripped the lead rope from my grip. Amazingly and uncannily, that lead rope whipped around behind him and went right up under his tail! It was the dang-dest thing I've ever seen, and I probably couldn't get a rope to do that again if I tried.

The big fella clamped his tail at first, and I was thinking

RC, the Thoroughbred who ripped the lead rope out of my hands and had it whip around up under his tail. (Photo: Carol Moates)

in that instant, "Oh boy...." But then he simply geared down, stopped, relaxed his tail, the rope fell out from under his tail and hit the ground, and he just stood there looking at me.

I have never been so glad I took the time to poke around and get a spot of worry worked out of a horse as I was with that one that day. I have no doubt that with as much anxiety as he had about that rope under the tail deal at first, and with the worry coming up in him about being asked to canter, that if we hadn't worked on it, he easily could have run through the panels or tried to jump over the panels, and in a complete panic really hurt himself.

One photo accompanying this chapter is of me working with my horse Jubal to get him better with a rope around his butt while Harry Whitney is coaching me from the side line at a clinic many years ago. Jubal had a tremendous fear of ropes when I got him, and that under the tail deal was a real flash-point. It got tons better at the clinic, and working on it put in my mind just one more spot where a horse person might go poking around looking for trouble with a horse before it gets big. Boy, am I glad for that one!

Being Particular

Here I am getting very particular in my presentation to step Cookie up onto a tire in the playground at Harry Whitney's place in Salome, Arizona. (Photo: Harry Whitney Horsemanship)

One of the greatest lessons that I have learned about working with horses—and one that I find to be of tremendous benefit to pass on to others as I teach horsemanship—is to be *very particular* in how we make requests of horses and in the results that we expect from those requests.

Particular-ness gets glossed over all too easily by us humans because we often overlook seemingly insignificant things that our horses don't miss or consider insignificant. Thus, we inadvertently teach horses things we wish we hadn't.

One example is allowing a horse's attention to drift off when we do something as simple as put on a halter or lead a horse from one place to another. If we allow horses to "disappear" mentally in the small details of our relationships then we are in essence teaching them that it is fine to ignore us. When this gets to be a habit, we shouldn't be surprised when they ignore us in other potentially more disconcerting areas, as well.

It was horsemanship clinician Harry Whitney who first made me aware that I was missing a great deal by not being nearly particular enough in my horse work. The root of the matter was that I was not noticing many moments when my horse left me mentally. In other words, I was not being particular enough at keeping my horse "with me" in all that we did together. Suffice it to say that I had no clue that I was being sloppy in my work, especially as hard as I was working to be on target with my feel, timing of releases, and such things that go into establishing good communication with horses.

In many of my books I share one of my favorite quotes from Harry: "Until you see it, you can't see it; then when you do see it, you wonder how you never saw *that* before!"

It is a quote that certainly applies to being particular with horses. We can overlook opportunities to improve our horse work by simply not paying close attention and noticing where we let a horse begin to run off the rails in seemingly insignificant ways. But when the situation escalates and we get a foot stepped on, can't get a horse in a trailer, or get bucked off, we see those more obvious challenges and can be quite motivated to work on them.

If we become more particular as a rule, it goes a long way towards keeping our horses mentally with us more of the time. This can shape up our work with horses to a much more refined state, even if we weren't having "big" troubles before. And if we manage not to miss those little moments where our horses' minds start to leave us and can keep them focused with us, then we even may find that some bigger problems simply evaporate.

Catherine Millard gets particular with HC when opening a gate.

So, enough theory. What does being more particular with a horse look like in the real world?

Let's take an occurrence that I often see as an example: a person begins some ground work by asking a horse to go and walk in a circle around her or him. But, the horse crowds the person, and perhaps even throws a shoulder in towards the person during the circling. If I am teaching and see this, I often will have the person stop and set the horse up to begin the circling again. Then, I point out the little details that are there to be seen before the horse runs amuck to help bring about an awareness in the horse handler to help to correct the problem.

Commonly what transpires is this. Things begin with

the person and the horse standing and facing each other. Next, the person walks around to the side of the horse to get into a position that places the horse where he should be relative to the person when on the circle.

Wait! Hold it right there. Already we have trouble.

Why do humans accommodate the horse in this way? Why do we feel the need to go and put ourselves into a correct position for the horse to circle around us? Why not simply ask the horse to move his feet, pivot on his hind feet, and step his front end laterally over away from us to get himself into the correct position to circle around us?

If the person walks around the horse to begin the circling, the horse can be standing there in a coma and it works out just peachy. The horse need not mentally or physically make a single minute motion towards participating in what we are initiating if we move to see that the horse is in the right spot to begin our circle.

So, I coach the person to begin again (horse and human standing facing each other), but to stand still this time and ask the horse to go and get into position on the circle rather than the other way around.

Most often what happens next is that the person remains standing still in front of the horse, but then the person takes the lead rope in the hand of the desired direction for the horse to begin circling and reaches out 90 degrees to the side, takes the slack out of the rope, and then begins to walk backwards. This pulls the horse forward and inevitably leads the horse right down the lead rope into the undesirable position of crowding the person, which is what we are working to fix in the first place.

Now it's time to see in our example how getting particular makes a huge difference in horsemanship. The next step is to explain that horses can follow a feel that a person presents on a lead rope, even a slack lead rope, but only if they are mentally available to us.

How do we keep a horse from crowding us when going

Harry Whitney uses feel on the lead rope to direct a mule to circle him as I look on in rapt attention. (Photo: Harry Whitney Horsemanship)

onto a circle? By not allowing it. How do we not allow it? By getting so particular from the very beginning of our requests that the right things work out so well that the horse gets supported through the process, finds releases in the correct moments, and voila! happy horse and happy person.

But this seems to be the really hard bit for many people. What needs to happen first is that the horse's mind must be centered on the person. If that is not the case and the horse's mind in AWOL, then the person needs to do something to get the horse awake and checking in. I often slap my chap with the end of the lead rope to make a noise, kick some sand, or perhaps use a flag to accomplish this. The point is that without the horse's mind focused on the handler, there can be no success because the horse will not be attentive to the request nor respond thoughtfully to it.

This is an aha! moment for some people, and one where Harry's quote above applies. Until it is pointed out, many folks have no idea that their horses are ignoring them at this stage. I often see horses looking off in the distance, sniffing the dirt, or glazed-over rather than being focused on the person on the other end of the lead rope. Some experienced horses may even be offering some of the motions that are being asked of them by the human but with an auto-pilot response lacking any thoughtful participation on the horses' part.

But when a person starts to see that a horse is completely out-to-lunch and how much better things go when they get a horse's attention and then make a request, it seems so obvious that they wonder how in the world they missed it.

Once the horse is focused, the second bit is to offer a feel for the horse to follow. In our scenario here, this amounts to the person offering that the horse step the front end laterally away. This can not happen if the horse comes forward, but rather the horse must be balanced or perhaps even rock back onto the hindquarters to pivot on the hind and step the front over to one side.

Another interesting aspect of this part is that it is not possible for a person to take the slack out of the lead rope and at the same time be asking a horse to step his front end over away from the person. If the person is in front of and facing the horse, the horse's front end must step laterally away from the person to get the horse into a position of being perpendicular to the person to be properly on the circle. Once in that position, if the horse walks forward he is on the circle.

There must be slack in the lead rope for the horse to have room to step his front end away from the person. Therefore, the person must leave plenty of slack in the rope and offer only a feel for the horse to follow to step the front end "over there" away from the person to one side.

All this detail may seem like an awful lot of busy-ness going on to get a horse to simply go around a person in a circle.

Yes! Yes it is. And that's the point. The more particular we are with even the most basic things we ask of our horses the more attentive and refined our horses become which in turn enhances their performance and their relationship with us.

It can take some time and effort on the person's part to break down every little thing we want to accomplish with our horses into minute parts and get each one polished up. But once that time is spent (and what might it be in the big picture, really; an hour, a day, maybe a week for some things?), the sum total can be a horse who then spends an entire lifetime with the wonderful habits of being attentive and willingly following a person. Such a horse is a joy work with and well worth the effort.

A note of caution on being particular (sidebar).

In getting educated about being particular, Harry pointed out to me that there is a big difference between being particular and picking at your horse in a micromanaging kind of way. If a person nit-picks a horse to death, the horse is likely going to become increasingly frustrated and desire to take his attention away from such a person.

This is avoided by getting clear changes in what one asks of a horse. If a horse is looking way over yonder when it is time to go out and circle a person, for example, do something like slap the end of the lead rope on the ground—do not do it *to* the horse (do not threaten, punish, or drive the horse), but rather make the ruckus in the environment around you—and this should get him to let go of his other thought and draw his attention to see what is happening there with you.

When the horse checks in, make that a nice quiet sweet spot between you two. Then offer what you have in mind to do with the horse and get going with it.

By contrast, do not stand there and do a bunch of little things to try and make a horse pay attention without really getting a solid focus. A person must get big enough to really get a horse's thought focused with him and then let that work out rather than just picking, and picking, and picking at the horse asking for focus but without really getting a meaningful change.

Opinion: That Horse Needs A Skilled Rider

Harry Whitney riding Kumi at Mendin' Fences Farm in Rogersville,
Tennessee where he does a run of clinics every spring.

Sometimes a horse person says something that hits me like moldy spot in a bale of decent hay and I'm not quite sure why. I have to ruminate a while to figure out just what is off about it and why it bugs me. I recently had one of these instances when I heard a horse person comment that a horse being discussed was a "more difficult" horse and thus required a "higher skill level rider."

Well, why should that trip me up? It makes sense, right? A difficult horse may need a capable rider. But, there's something about this idea and what is meant by it that isn't always so cut-and-dry.

Chewing on the somewhat sour reaction I experienced got me to thinking that this notion bothers me because in some scenarios it indicates what I consider to be a wrong way of thinking.

Sometimes, as was the case with the example above, what people are saying is that the horse is in sorry shape mentally. For that reason the horse requires a rider able to "handle" a tense, worried horse to get such a horse to do the things the person wants to do in spite of the angst and tension in the horse.

That usage has quite a different meaning than saying something I would agree with, like that an advanced jumping horse requires someone with some decent jumping skills to safely go out and jump. These are two different ideas.

It would be great if what was being meant was: "This horse needs someone who has enough experience and handiness getting horses feeling better about things with people as to be able to bring the relationship with a horse to a better spot so the horse can be ridden and do tasks with increasing relaxation and general okay-ness." It's a long sentence, but it works for me. And often, it is not what is meant.

Another oddity that comes to my mind when considering this peeve I stumbled onto is that in actuality, a less "experience/skilled" rider may be the one who possesses the abilities in superior quantities to get a horse to feel better about things.

This person probably will not be the one who is willing to march the horse around mechanically—holding a horse in check whose mind is outside the immediate space wishing he was somewhere else.

Willingness comes into play here. The idea of a willing partner in a horse is incongruent with the image of a horse tight as a fiddle string from tension being handled by a "skilled" rider—a rider who is skilled at making a horse do something when it is not at all what that horse wants to be doing at that moment.

It's pretty clear to see that the better a horse feels, the better he or she performs, and the easier it becomes for the rider to ask for and receive willingness in actions from the horse. A horse more advanced in this way of being handled (with a more willing and less stressful relationship to the human) ought to be less difficult to ride. Or to say it this way: a horse more advanced in being present and willing and relaxed with the rider should be safer and more available for even a novice horseperson to ride in general.

Obviously, as stated earlier, a person who never has jumped a horse before shouldn't be expected to get on an experienced jumping horse to go jump a course without any training. So, I get that.

But, notice that it is when people say that a more skilled rider is needed because "the horse is" difficult, or advanced, or whatever, that it bothers me—not when people say that the activity we are asking the horse to do requires a more skilled rider.

Part of the issue that I have here, it seems, is that the very goal of what some folks are speaking about is that the things they expect the "difficult" horse to do are THE goal. In other words, if their intention is simply to ride the horse and do some task—whatever it is from trail riding, to jumping, to cow work, to dressage, to whatever—then that is THE focus. And they are saying that the horse requires a rider who can make that happen even though the horse is reluctant and "acts up." That's what flips my flapjack wrong-side up.

On the other hoof, if the very goal of a rider is to get a horse feeling better about doing things with a person, then that requires a whole different attitude and aptitude from the rider. It requires a horsemanship that looks to increase relaxation and willingness in a horse when accomplishing the tasks that a person wants to do with the horse.

Having In Mind
What You Want To
Ask Your Horse

*Chief and me on the farm road where we worked on getting him to
lead in a relaxed way. (Photo: Carol Moates)*

It's not uncommon for the poor response of a horse to a person's request to be due in large part to the person not really being certain what she or he wants the horse to do.

"Uh, Tom," you might say, "just how is it that you think that a person can request things of a horse without having those things in mind first?"

It's a fair question. The truth is, plenty of people "sorta" ask their horses to do things. These convoluted, haphazard requests asked of horses are not intentionally made so. They do, however, have very real repercussions and a big bearing on the nature of the relationship between horses and humans.

My horsemanship mentor Harry Whitney is fond of saying, "Until you see it, you can't see it; and then when you do see it, you wonder how you never saw THAT before!" This is one of those kind of things.

When we lack clarity in our human minds as to what exactly we'd like a horse to do, then there is no possible way for the horse to know exactly what to do. Lack of clarity in the horse's world is not a good thing. Horses take great comfort in knowing where things stand with other beings (especially other horses and humans) and within their environment. When we provide consistency and clarity as to what is expected of horses when we make requests of them then they can gain confidence—both in precisely what they need to do and that things will turn out okay if they follow our lead. It is only when horses feel confident in our requests that they are able to accomplish those tasks with relaxation, and even willingness.

Recently, I had a rather discouraged student who was struggling to get her horse to quit "being a spaz." When leading the horse, the horse crowded her and tended to dance around. But the owner walked along without truly guiding and checking in with her horse. Once the horse got to dancing around, the owner got nervous. Finally, the owner erupted into bursts of bigness when she'd had enough shenanigans. It was a pendulum swinging back and forth between the horse running amuck as the person sorta tried to lead the horse in a direction, and the human's somewhat angry outbursts that caused the horse finally to take real notice of her, if only for a few moments. Then back it swung again the other way.

The horse's mind was all over the place, causing the trouble, but in observing the owner, the human's mind also was not focused on what she really wanted the horse to do, likewise causing the trouble. This situation offered no chance for the horse to relax because the person was not offering guidance and boundaries to be followed. The mare never knew for sure that she was in the place she needed to be for things to be okay because the human was not establishing this. In the absence of capable guidance, the horse went about doing the best she could, taking matters into her own hoofs. And when the human finally got perturbed and biggish, that only added to the tension in the horse because it added to the confusion and was not used to establish a more permanent means of keeping the horse mentally on track going forward with direction.

In this instance, I pointed out how the owner was wanting the horse to follow along and not act up, but that such a general presentation alone didn't provide the support the horse needed to know where and how to be. A little coaching to get the owner to think more precisely about where she wanted the horse to be, and then to keep track of her horse with each step, showed improvement. And when the horse began to "act up" again, the owner began to realize that she (the owner) had indeed slipped away mentally and not taken care of directing her horse to the extent necessary to keep the mare with her and feeling more relaxed.

People fail at times to understand how close to the surface a horse's self preservation instincts reside. If a horse isn't certain of where things stand at any given moment with interactions with a human, the horse can feel the need to take control of the situation. This can be a powerful need within a horse.

In a way, there is hardly a more simple task to undertake

with horses than leading them, but it is not uncommon to see people really struggle with this. And such a simple task reveals the very nature of the relationship between the horse and human. Two people may take the same horse, the same lead rope, and go along the same path and have entirely different results. The reason for the horse leading calmly and willingly or the opposite often results from the human's presentation.

On the first hand, we have a person who knows he wants to lead a horse from point A to point B. He walks holding the horse's lead rope, but he is thinking about his truck needing the oil changed, that he's out of milk at home, and, oh yeah, that when they get to the arena over there that he's going to work on walk-to-trot transitions.... Hey horse! What're'ya doing? Get back there behind me—hey, stop crowding me!

On the other hand, here's a fella who leaves point A and is not only attentive to each step as they set off, but is thinking about exactly where he wants the horse to be in relation to him. This person offers a feel, say, for the horse to be a little off to his left side, for the horse's head to be a foot behind him, and for the horse to be thinking forward along in the direction that the two are walking. This person has in his mind exactly what he expects the horse to do and offers this "place" for the horse to be as a very sweet spot between them where the horse can be fully confident that things are rosy and safe. The moment this person feels an imbalance between himself and the horse, he is getting busy in some way to indicate to the horse that the diversion isn't going to work out. This can be something as little as a soft feel on the rope or a sound made as a precursor to a larger "correction." Getting bigger can be actions like slapping a chap with the end of the lead rope or stopping and backing the horse until the horse's mind is present with the person and on task again—but not so excessively big that more worry is put into the horse.

And the big benefit is that once a person begins to establish this kind of rapport with the horse, it can become the very nature of the relationship between the human and the horse.

The understanding that the person offers a "place" for the horse to be—a little to the side and behind when being led, between the human's reins and legs when being ridden, looking in a certain direction when being asked with a feel on the lead rope, whatever it is—can be understood, expected, and the norm.

An interesting aspect of all this is that horses who are distracted are more tense and troubled. This is due to the fact that horses having strong thoughts elsewhere wish to carry them out and a human is in the way of that. Whereas, horses who have been brought along to let go of their own strong thoughts and are able to follow the human's lead are the ones who relax and even become willing to undertake tasks directed by people.

Some years ago I had an experience that provided me a solid illustration of this truth, and I shared it with my student mentioned above to help explain the point I was hoping to make to her. When we got Chief, my wife Carol's Paint stallion, he was living in a paddock on one side of the farm. The horse was being walked along a farm road about a quarter mile to graze another field each day. Once through the gate, Chief's MO was to holler, head held high, and with eyes looking everywhere but where he was being led. He was a handful. I decided to work on it.

I began by choosing to check in with Chief continually to see how far he could follow along with the feel I presented before his mind went AWOL and the misfit adventures got rolling. I discovered, to my surprise, that it was every-single-step! The horse could not take a step without losing the plot and having his thought drift away, and in a big way. I would stop and ask with some feel on the lead rope for him to check in, and at first he was so oblivious that he just tried to march right past me. I'd put a big flip in the rope to interrupted his other interests, and his head would shoot up. I'd back him up, which took some pretty big action on the lead rope, and get his attention and then have him focus carefully on what I had in mind for us to do— namely to take a single step forward and not leave me mentally. It took forever before I got even one decent step where he could manage to stay with me, relax, and be where I had in mind for him to be when stepping forward.

It was a huge workout. First, I finally got that one decent step—I had begun to wonder if our journey would make it only the first five feet that day! Then the stallion managed two steps without "acting up." Then, three. It took us 45 minutes to walk along the farm road from point A to point B doing what it took to keep him with me and not blowing all over the place mentally—that trip was typically just a 10 minute stroll.

The next day, I set out with Chief with the same intent. Right at the beginning it looked just as bad as the previous day and the horse went AWOL with every single step. But, I soon discovered that the stallion came through to a better spot with my interventions more quickly than the day before. It only took us 30 minutes to make the trip that day.

The next day was even quicker, and by the fourth day, we were doing it in 10 minutes, easy, and without any fuss whatever. At that point, it was easy to feel if Chief was not tracking right with me and was about to go AWOL. And if he began to stray, all I had to do was to put a little feel on the lead rope and he let go whatever his distraction was and he came right back into the sweet spot with me. He did this because he knew from experience that getting distracted wasn't going to work out—that I would stop and deal with his distracted thoughts until he let them go, so why even go there? And, it surely felt better to him to be relaxed and following along in a smooth way with me than to be all upset and tense. To this day, many years later, Chief remains super easy to lead and those handful of difficult sessions proved to be time well spent.

At first, it may seem like a major hassle to get a horse's attention and keep it for every single step of a journey. But, a couple of hours over a few days with Chief has led to more than a decade of easy leading. And, had there been no human intervention, that stallion still would be running amuck and feeling extreme tension when being led today.

Ever since that bit of work early on to get Chief leading nicely he's been easy to lead and follows along willingly. (Photo: Carol Moates)

The more clearly we foresee just where we want our horses to be when we ask something of them, the better chance they have of finding that sweet spot with us. And when we get really particular about it—coupled with actions that are big enough to help horses let go of their distracted thoughts and tense feelings and search out what we are asking—they can become confident in us and our directing. This helps develop a relationship of willingness that can spread to all areas with our horses.

Ground Work

Harry Whitney gets a soft and relaxed feel going between a young mare and himself, even with his close contact on the knot of the rope halter—they clearly have some with-you-ness going on at this moment.

Ground work—the art of working a horse afoot—often takes a back seat to riding. It's understandable; people typically fall in love with horses with the foremost desire to spend their time riding them. But, good ground work can be hugely beneficial to building the kind of riding relationship many horse owners strive to achieve with their horses.

Horsemanship, in my mind, is the skill of setting up the relationship between the horse and the human. If the relationship is right, then we have a horse who thinks along with our requests. Rather than a mechanical endeavor, like pulling on a rein, the relationship can be based on a true communication where a slight feel put on a rein with a finger is all it takes to have a horse think in a direction and go there willingly.

"All ground work is a way of checking in to see if the horse is mentally with us," horsemanship clinician Harry Whitney says. "So, what you do is not as important as how you go about doing it, and whether you're attentive to where your horse's mind is. So, your ground work could be done by the time you get a horse caught, led to the barn, groomed, and saddled. In that time, if you know your horse is with you mentally, you just go on, but if he's not, you might be glad you did a little ground work before riding."

Often folks regard ground work merely as a series of exercises, but the importance of ground work isn't in particular exercises. Simply drilling a horse on exercises won't achieve the desired relationship results if we neglect to consider where the horse's mind is focused along the way.

The truth is, we really don't teach horses how to do things. If you've ever seen horses get down on one knee to grab a mouthful of grass from under a fence you can see they already physically have the ability to bow. Humans can train horses to bow on request, but we simply are asking them to do something that they already are capable of. The same is true of circling, backing, trotting...but what is important is that we sort it out so that horses understand our requests and then perform such tasks with a willingness because they feel good and relaxed about doing them with us. Ground work is a great way to set up this kind of rapport.

Harry coined the phrase "with-you-ness" to refer to what might be called the ultimate refined form between the horse and the human. I was delighted to grasp this concept when I first heard Harry share it at a clinic years ago. I wrote it down word-for-word, and later shared a whole chapter on it in the book *A Horse's Thought*. That definition is:

"A way of the horse and human each responding to the other while participating in the same experience--both aware of, and being sensitive to, the mental desires, emotional balance, as well as physical needs of the other, during which time there is no fear, anxiety, resistance, or resentment."

So, in whatever we ask of our horses, if we first pay attention to where they are paying attention and then do the work to redirect their focus if it is wayward to get it with us, then we are setting them up to win and make meaningful changes for the better in all we do with them. It is helpful to train yourself to observe when a horse is heading down the trail to trouble from the moment you fetch him from the field or stall, put a halter on him, lead him from here to there, and so on.

You can use most any ground work activity as a with-you-ness barometer and to get your horse more attentive if he isn't. We can use backing as an example. Ask a horse to back straight away from you a few steps, stop, and remain in that new spot standing relaxed and calm. What a horse presents when you try a bit of ground work like this provides insight into his mental state and tells much about if he can follow a feel presented by a person, leave other thoughts so he can follow along with the request, and be settled about it.

Often when I work with someone for the first time I'll ask the person to back a horse with the lead rope. People com-

Mirage follows the feel I present and is with me as I work on directing her thought in the ground work from a position back a ways where the rider will sit. (Photo: Carol Moates)

monly respond by approaching the horse, taking a tight hold of the lead rope close under the halter, and pushing the rope towards the horse's chest. I then ask the person to back the horse while standing in front of the horse without stepping towards the horse. Someone who is unfamiliar with sending a feel up the lead rope will be unsure about how to accomplish the task and a little coaching is needed.

The first point to understand is how to make a request of a horse. Harry says it simply, "Begin where you want to end up." So to ask the horse to back, begin by putting the feel for the horse to back up on the lead rope in the way you would like it to be in your perfect reality. For me, that is an almost imperceiveably light up-and-down wiggle on the rope. At first, a horse who isn't used to this won't understand it and may not pay much attention to me. However, horses don't miss much and even though they don't yet have a frame of reference for that slight feel on the lead rope, it needs to be there to give them the chance to hear it and act on it.

A sensitive horse might step back almost immediately. A not-so-sensitive horse might stand there not even making an attempt to search for what you're presenting until you get very active with that lead rope. But in all cases, when the horse begins to think about the situation and try something different it is time to release your "ask" on the rope. Horses learn from this release—they desire that sweet spot of balance with a person and prefer to avoid escalation in the presentation. If you are consistent with handling it, they begin to hunt for the answer to what you are asking in all the different kinds of requests you make of them.

There is an important point to consider here—where the hoof really hits the highway regarding the true relationship between a horse and a human—which is that one must watch out to make certain that the horse begins to *think* backwards as we build on our humble beginnings to get him to step back.

If I ask the horse to back and he takes a reverse step but his mind has not yet let go of going forward, then the moment I release for his backwards step he may be coming forward again. If he is unable to stand relaxed after backing, then he has not really thought about going backwards. He hasn't let go of thinking about going forwards even though I managed to get his body to move back a step. He may have gone backwards to avoid the pressure that is applied, but he wasn't going along with the feel I presented and really thinking backwards—and there is a big difference between these two things.

When a horse thinks about going backwards (or doing anything, for that matter), he will show commitment to the task. If we offer the slightest hint for the horse to back with a feel on the lead rope and he does so with his head low and a softness, that's a pretty good indication he's happy to back and thinking backwards. If we do not get through to the horse's mind with an ask and truly get a change of thought, then we haven't accomplished what we intended to and we won't experience a true willingness and with-you-ness with the horse.

Put another way, I don't simply want my horse to back when I ask. I want my horse to hear my slightest ask, be backing readily and wholeheartedly, and have no tension in doing it. As I work on backing in the work, I will begin to hold out on giving a release if all these criteria aren't coming through until they do. So a step backwards won't get a release from me pretty soon in the work if the horse's head is up and he is stiff as a board. In that case I will continue with my ask until he not only steps back but the head comes down and he softens which happens only when he starts to *think* backwards with me.

I could go on for volumes about the many nuances and applications of ground work and what a great tool it is to develop our relationship to horses. But, the crux of the matter is that the underlying principle to achieve with-you-ness always points back to where the horses' attentions are focused.

Harry says, "The best thing we can do for our horses is get them into the habit of letting go of a thought." If we become aware of when horses aren't truly with us and then get them to let go of their thoughts in the ground work to come along with what we present as a general bases for all interactions in those relationships, then that togetherness will carry over into the riding. It becomes a way of life between us, and the best benefit of all is how relaxed and willing our equine companions can become at all times when we interact with them.

Is It Physical or Mental

(Photo: Judy Thomas)

The question of whether a horse issue is rooted in a physical problem or a "mental" one (i.e., a training issue) comes up fairly often in my horsemanship clinics and lessons. Asking, "is an issue physical or mental?" is a very important question because helping a horse through a problem really depends on getting an accurate answer to it up front.

First, I suppose it is somewhat obvious that if there indeed is a physical issue causing a problem with a horse then that ailment overrides any horsemanship answers to the problem. Something inflicting pain on a horse (ailments like kissing spine, laminitis, ulcers, etc.) consume the horse's moments, and relief (when possible) must come from medical treatment and/or convalescence.

Sometimes one may be able to get to the bottom of an issue and understand a certain physical cause for a problem. For instance, I have witnessed issues with a horse being ridden that when the saddle was pulled and fingers were carefully pressed along either side of the spine under where the saddle had set, the horse suddenly winced when a sore spot was discovered. Rest a horse like that, or do some ground work with him and don't ride, and the soreness and problems caused by it should disappear in time. Likewise, a horse with dental issues may "misbehave" when the reins are engaged if a bit is used. These kinds of things do happen, and it is good to mark them off the list first when exploring the reasons for a horse problem since physical problems will override any other work we hope to accomplish with the horse.

On the other hand, many horse troubles (perhaps even most horse troubles I run across)—and many horse issues that may seem to be all or in part of a physical nature at first—can be totally mental. This is the realm where good horsemanship makes a difference, and sometimes the improvements can be profound.

The above mention of a horse presenting with some issues when the reins and a bit are used is a good one to start with. I often see horses flip their heads and chomp their bits when tacked out for work. Sometimes, just putting the bridle on the horse is enough to get that chomping the bit trouble brewing without the reins even being touched. Many times people ask me about this kind of behavior in a horse, and often there is a concern that it may be a physical issue in the horse's mouth. What I typically find as that the underlying trouble lies with how the reins have been handled with the horse.

One very telling test is to put a side pull with reins on the horse so that there is no bit. If a person goes to use the reins with the side pull and the horse demonstrates the same kind of reaction as he did when there was a bit, it's not a dental issue. Head flipping and even the chomping can still occur with an empty mouth, and this is stress related. Inconsistency with the use of the reins is often the root cause for this kind of trouble. The fix is to begin to use the reins differently.

Consistency is critical here. If the reins have been "sounding" like a bunch of static to the horse, that must be changed so that the reins communicate clear, concise messages. And, the consistency I speak of is that a rein always should be engaged to ask for the horse to think in a direction. Then a release should be given when the horse's thought comes through so that the horse will understand that he got the correct answer. I have witnessed nearly miraculous turn-arounds in horses who easily could have led one to think there was a dental issue but basic improvement in handling the reins cleared it up.

Another example can be found in how a horse carries himself. A horse can be ridden with such tension and tightness that he presents as stiff, braced, or even lame. A horse with head held high who is board straight and has rock hard muscles can show what might at first seem to be physical issues. Well, to be honest, they are physical issues—but ones brought on by stress and tension, and that can be alleviated or improved by how a horse is handled.

Put a different way, a horse can perform tasks in a me-

Harry Whitney and RC, a gelding who had me wondering more than once whether his issues were physical or mental...he had some of both.

chanical way and get them done but not feel good about them or have them look good. Regardless of what is being performed— jumping, racing, trail riding, cutting, dressage, roping—we can push a horse into doing things or we can work on our horseman-ship and see that the horse does not just perform these things, but does them in a relaxed way.

I often glean answers to horse problems from the lessons I've learned from my mentor Harry Whitney, and this is no exception. He often points out that a horse who isn't feeling his best can't perform his best. A horse going around full of tension is in no way feeling his best.

Whole volumes can be written on the topic of how to work on getting horses to be willing partners who perform well because they feel relaxed and good about things; I've actually written a bunch of them myself! But here, let's just boil that down and say, like with the reins example above, consistency in having a horse's attention and in how we ask a horse to perform certain tasks goes a long way to getting a more relaxed and willing partner in a horse.

I have seen horses at clinics who made such short choppy steps with their front legs that any onlooker thought for sure something physical was ailing the poor creatures. An hour later, the next day, or the day after that, depending on how things go at a clinic, these horse's could be moving like a million bucks. The horses' goose stepping issues resulted from their being so pinched up inside their minds that their bodies likewise became too tight to function properly, and some good horsemanship was able to alleviate some of that worry to the point that the horses could move more naturally again.

Presently, I am working with a Quarter Horse who is a very good example of this very scenario. When asked to turn around, if left to her own devices, the mare is so stiff that she will awkwardly hop her front end around and sometimes even stumble. It can make the rider wonder at first if she has something seriously wrong going on in her front end. But, if I work with her a few minutes concentrating on having her with me mentally, getting her to truly think around a turn, and maybe even do some other work like ask her to let go of the tension through her body and give me a leg yield or two, things change for the better. A change of mind results in a change in the body, and this also can bring about a change for the better in the relationship between a horse and a human.

By having a rein really engage the mare's mind to think around to a side rather than just causing her to fling some half-hearted turn at the rider while thinking off to some other distant thing, she becomes more willing to step that direction.

I can feel her think about the move when I ask for it, rock her weight back a bit, relax, and start to bend through her body more as she executes the turn. When she stops bracing mentally, you wouldn't think it was the same horse as before as she comes around very nicely in a bend.

When a problem arises with a horse, asking whether there is a physical or mental problem as the basis for it is really crucial to figuring out an effective way to address the issue. And there are so many variables it is hard to crystallize a way to cover this topic in an essay. Plus, to top it all off, it also can happen that a horse is showing some problems that are resulting from both some mental and physical problems. Hopefully, kicking around a few thoughts on the matter is helpful. It is important to keep an open mind on both ends to best help the horses in our care.

Handling Spooks on the Trail

(Photo: Danielle Gruber)

The thing about handling spooks on the trail is that the best way to deal with them is to do so before you ever leave home.

To put this in terms I have learned from many years of studying with horsemanship clinician Harry Whitney—if your horse is not in the habit of letting go of his thoughts to willingly go along with what you present at home, and you get into adverse conditions where your horse has a pretty strong thought, then you are going to be in trouble.

In other words, the best way to avoid having a wreck when something spooks your horse on the trail is to spend plenty of time in ideal conditions working on this with your horse. Experiment at home with some things to see how tenaciously your horse stays with a sidetracked thought when you ask for his attention.

As a simple example, imagine your horse is in a round pen. If another horse comes into sight, will your horse leave you mentally and focus on the other horse in such a strong way that you have difficulty getting his attention back? Set up a friend over in the bushes with a plastic bag to crinkle—can you become more important to your horse than that? You get the idea. If you can not get through to your horse in these kinds of scenarios at home where your horse ought to naturally feel the most confident then it is very unlikely your horse will be available to hear you when out in the wild country and something frightens him.

This situation is a bit like a parent trying to talk to a child who is engrossed in a favorite TV show. Sometimes the parent has to get pretty big to break the spell of a show so the child can hear what is being said. Get into the habit of looking for similar instances where your horse is not with you mentally. Learn to check in with your horse by asking in various way—like presenting a little feel on a lead rope or rein to see if the horse can soften and acknowledge you—to know if he is available for you to ask him to do a task.

If not, then do something just big enough to get the

horse's attention. You might slap your chap, kick the ground, scratch your jacket—whatever works to dislodge the horse's diverted thought is fine. But, do not do anything to the horse or direct anything at him to intentionally drive him. Instead, try to draw the horse's attention towards you. You need to be a bigger bugger then the one in the bushes. But when the horse checks you out, stop what you were doing and present a sweet spot to him so that coming to you mentally becomes very rewarding and comforting to the horse.

Getting into a routine of checking to see where your horse's mind is, and establishing the ability with your horse to let go of other thoughts when it is time to pay attention to you, will be cash money in large bills (metaphorically speaking, of course) if you find yourself on a trail and something spooky happens. Conversely, if you can not get your horse with you at home, then it is very unlikely you will succeed in doing so out there.

Regardless of all the best laid plans to prevent trail troubles by training ahead of riding out in the big wide world, we all realize that with horses spooks still can happen. When they do, if you've done your homework, hopefully your horse will be able to hear your input as a rider rather than just bolt in shear panic blocking you out completely. One of the most important and helpful bits of advice to follow when a spook happens is to keep your horse pointed towards whatever it is that is spooking him.

"Depending on the level of worry," Harry says, "you might need to let them stand there and look once you bend them back so that they can realize that it's not going to kill them. But if they're too worried, then you better let them move a little, but don't let them get their tail to it. Angle over here and over there, and get a little distance away from it."

This scenario is critical because a horse is hardwired to flee from fear, and they are supremely good at it. If a horse is spooked by something and turns so that it is behind him, his concern typically escalates to a panic and your horse may show you just how these critters stay alive in a pinch (by clearing a

My wife Carol's gelding Stoney and I cross a creek. It is easy to see Stoney's apprehension as we step out of the creek and pick up a road on the other side. (Photo: Danielle Gruber)

quarter mile faster than many other animals on the planet!). But, keep the horse facing the spooky thing the best you can and two helpful things happen.

First, it keeps the horse from fleeing forward, and if he tries fleeing backwards away from the booger it will be a whole lot slower and more manageable for the rider. The other thing is that the horse's mind will be more engaged to think about what is happening. He may be frightened by the spooky thing, but he will be forced to face it and see what it is and if it really is a horse eating monster or not. This is a much more preferable set up to a horse just bolting in a panic: scooting first and asking questions later.

This bit of advice also can be worked on at home.

"Program your mind to bend your horse back around towards the spook and try to keep his nose to it," Harry says. "So many times people go fetal and the horse takes off with them. If they had their minds programmed ahead of time, they maybe could have reacted in a way that got the horse bent around to start over, sorting things out, instead of hauling on both reins more like a race horse heading away from it."

Harry teaches that in a situation where a horse spooks, using one rein is far better than engaging both.

"If you panic and grab both reins," Harry says, "the horse can get straight as a board and have tremendous power. If they're resistant to one rein, then they are exponentially resistant to two reins. Not only does he have tremendous power then, but like I said, he'll lean into the bit just like a race horse on the track and away he goes. If they're that panicked and going that hard, you'd pick up one rein and try to get them bent by thinking to that one rein and start to come around to that side."

Harry warns not to haul the horse's head around because that can throw the horse off balance and tip him over—a move that is easy to see stunt riders do in many old western movies, but not a stunt you would like to see on a trail ride. You also must be mindful that if your horse is truly in a panic and bolting, if you pull his head around but he remains fleeing forward, he may not be able to see where he is going. That is when a horse runs into a tree or through a fence. Once a horse bolts, use one rein to try to get him to think about bending around to one side and then spiral him down slower and slower until he stops, if you can.

"I knew a woman," Harry says, "and she'd have four or

five children riding with her, and at any random moment she'd holler, 'Oh no!' Then they all bent their horses around to a stop. The point is that they were programming their minds to bend a horse if something suddenly happens. But the randomness of when she would do it was different than if we are doing it ourselves. You could do that with a friend, just riding along and your friend hollers 'Oh no!'"

And one more piece of advice...if you trail ride with others, your horse may not need to be the spooky one to have a spooking episode. If another horse spooks and bolts, other horses including yours may decide that leaving the area with the herd at a high rate of speed is the best plan.

"If you have the horse 'with you' instead of allowing him strictly to be going with the other horses then you can avoid this," Harry says. "A lot of horses are just going down the trail with another horse. So, if the other horse disappears, then your horse is going to disappear, too."

The "with you" that Harry refers to points back to where this discussion began. Having a horse who is capable of letting go of strong diverted thoughts and is capable of being "with" the rider in a mental sense is one who can be most effectively supported when something unexpected happens.

Vaccinating Dinky

Dinky the Mule. (Photo: Dianne Madden)

Many of you readers may fondly remember Dinky the Mule who's exploits have graced a handful of chapters in my books. Dinky proved to be a very troubled fella who had very good reasons to be from what is known of his past poor experiences with humans. Dinky's current owners Dianne and Pat Madden have worked with me for years to help alleviate some of Dinky's worries. And although we have helped him make some profound changes for the better, there remain some flash points for Dinky that can send him into a dangerous flight-or-fight fit of panic. One of the worst of those triggers is getting vaccinated.

The epic episodes of hazardous meteoric panic Dinky expresses when the vet goes to give him his shots became legendary with Pat and Dianne, and clearly with their vets, as well. This mule provides an extreme example of a horrific reaction to vet handling. But the experience I want to share here from yesterday of administering vaccines to Dinky also provides an example of an important point—that some consideration for the equine coupled with an application of decent horsemanship can make a massive difference for the better. And that difference can be felt by the mule (or horse or donkey), the owners, and the vet.

I'd offered to give Dinky his shots after hearing the way things went year after year. Dianne and Pat have a good relationship with their vet but they were cautious to say, "Hey, let our trainer give the shots." They thought it sounded as much like a criticism as an offer for help. But Dianne was unable to sleep for several nights before the vet was scheduled to arrive to vaccinate just knowing how terribly Dinky would react and what Dinky would be subjected to to get the job done. Namely, that he ended up being tied to a post along a fence where he would kick, rear, pitch himself nearly to the ground, kick some more, and strike at anyone during the deal, and so forth. It was a horrible scenario, and as Dianne articulated to me, a setback to the work she had been doing to help Dinky for so long. But it also is important to her that Dinky have proper health care, so she was in quite a quandary. She wanted to get a change in this situation but felt stuck with it. But this year the scales of her terrible anticipation tipped to the point that she asked the vet to provide the vaccines so that I might have a go at administering them. It seems that the vet was more than happy to oblige.

I suspect one of the worst aspects for Dianne, too, was that she felt like she was betraying Dinky's trust every year when vaccination time rolled around. And this is a woman who has dedicated significant time and money to helping Dinky feel better about people and his surroundings. She really cares.

I want to be fair to veterinarians at this point and point out that it's not the vets' job to train horses (or mules). That's our responsibility as owners, and if we do our job well then hopefully it'll go better for the animals and the vets when they must interact. However, that's not to say that vets and the equines they treat wouldn't benefit from doing the job with a little horsemanship in mind. This can set things up to be better for the horse and vet, and to make future farm calls less difficult. And to be truthful, I wasn't sure I could get Dinky any better about taking shots than what the vets had done, but I had an idea that I could and was willing to give it a go.

To speak to vets directly for a minute; I get that part of the dynamic is that, of course, time is money. Like any worker getting paid by the job, as a vet, you want to get the job done and get on to the next call. And there can be pressure to get to emergency calls and still get to all the regularly scheduled visits in a day, and so forth. But my experience with Dinky yesterday proves that taking the time it takes to set things up better for the mule actually can take less time—sometimes, far less time. And even if it took more time the first time (which I'll explain below wasn't the case yesterday, but easily could have), it is likely to save time in the future. This surely would be an asset for any vet in those cases where the owner has not been capable of better preparing a horse for handling.

So, soap box aside, here's what happened with Dinky just as an example of an extreme case of a terrified mule with a proven track record of presenting serious problems when being vetted, given shots in a way that worked out so much better that it's uncanny.

Dinky is a companion to Dianne's Walking Horse, Rowdy. When I went out, I trimmed both of those guys first—and trimming Dinky has been a many years' long endeavor to get to the point where I can do it with relative safety. That all went like usual yesterday and Dinky remained relaxed through it. Then Rowdy was put in a stall in the barn and I led Dinky up close to him in the aisle way so there was a stall wall between them, but they were close through the bars. I figured the equine companionship might help Dinky relax a little.

My main focus was to get Dinky as relaxed as possible. This would help generally, but specifically, if his neck muscles were not rock hard then the shot would hurt him less. I figured that in the past by the time the vet was ready with the shots and Dinky was confined and fighting as hard as he could that those neck muscles were like plates of armor to penetrate.

Dinky settled there, so I began poking him with my thumb in the neck area where the shot would go. I had the lead rope draped loosely over my left arm with a loop of slack going to the halter. He settled into that easily enough. Then I took a syringe with the plastic cap still covering the needle and poked him with that on the neck. He didn't get too worried about that, so I was glad to see that the sight and sound of the syringe was not a problem. Then a took my knife off my belt, opening it up, and started poking him with the tip so that the point of the blade pricked him a little. He took plenty of notice of that and got wide-eyed, but managed to stay there with me. I poked with the knife tip until he started to relax, then I quit for a minute, and repeated that until he was standing very quietly. Next, I pulled the cap off the needle and began pricking him with it in the same general area. He took more offence to this than anything I had done so far, but within a couple of minutes, he began to relax with that, too.

It was time, and I wasn't at all sure if I was about to get knocked flat and run the length of with little mule feet or not...so I positioned myself, kept pricking and pricking, and then...zip. It

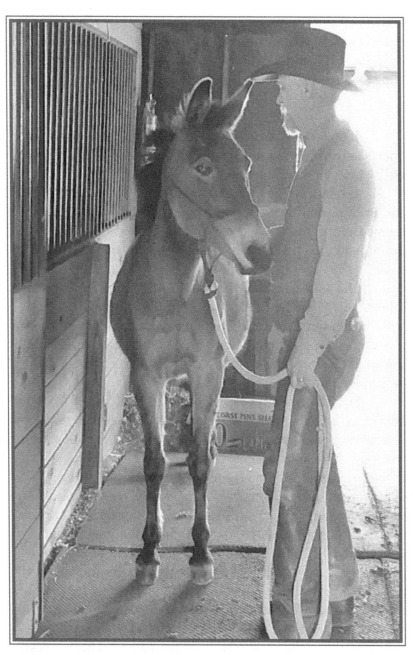

This photo was snapped by Dianne as I was in the poking mode before giving Dinky the first shot. (Photo: Dianne Madden)

was done. Dinky jumped a little at the full-on shot but he never pitched a fit or became overly bothered. I looked at Dianne, and she looked at me like, "Well, what did you stop for?"

"That's it," I said.

"You gave it to him already?" she asked. "That was it?"

"Yep."

It was so quick and uneventful she had missed seeing it. Then she handed me another syringe, and I thought, "Oh great... well, lets see how this one goes."

I went through the same warm-up with the poking and pricking and I got the same results, although I'd say Dinky jumped a little bit more when I gave the second shot. Still, no drama, and then the mule just stood there and let me remove his halter.

The whole business took about 10 minutes. Dianne had told me that it had taken at least 45 minutes to terrorize Dinky with the more conventional method of vaccinating used when the vet came to do it and that it was extremely dangerous. Plus, the last time Dinky had injured a hind leg in the process and limped for a few days.

Since then, I just keep thinking about it. I keep thinking how much a little understanding and perhaps even less time investment up front goes into getting things better for our critters when we apply some decent horsemanship and consideration to the equation. As humans (owners, vets, trainers, farriers—all of us who interact with equines), we have the tendency to want to make things happen with animals and to confine the animals into taking what we want to do with them. But if we think a little about how to get them to relax and put a bit of time into preparing them for things like getting shots or having their feet handled, everything can go so much better and such experiences can be no more worrisome than many others that they experience with us humans. I relate to Dinky, and I was happy to do unto him as I would want done unto me if I was in his hooves.

The Round Pen

When I began my horsemanship journey, one thing I noticed right away was that most everybody seemed to be using round pens. I figured there must be something pretty special about this particular kind of horse containment.

Observing and working with horsemanship clinician Harry Whitney early on in my journey is what brought me to understand that all round-penning is not created equal. Comprehending the why of that fact can be hugely beneficial when working to gain a better relationship and communication with a horse.

Boiled down, the biggest hinge-point in horsemanship is whether or not a person gets through to a horse's mind and thereby gets a horse truly with her or him or not. The opposite of that is to get "mechanical" actions from a horse whereby the horse is not truly mentally with the person but is just going through, or being driven into, motions.

There is a huge difference between these two. To someone uninitiated with the idea of getting a horse truly mentally focused, round pen work might seem to look the same if done either way. There's a person in the middle of the round pen and the horse goes around her or him this way or that way. But

Harry Whitney works a young mare in the round pen at his place in Salome, Arizona.

when the nuances that are going on between a person and a horse in the round pen become apparent, the set-up can provide a fabulous example of the difference between a horse being driven into actions (or on auto pilot) and one who is following a feel presented by a person.

First, it might be worth noting that I discovered that there is no magic in the round pen itself. Yes, round pens are nice. I have one myself. They are very handy to work a horse in, particularly at liberty, where the horse has freedom to move around while remaining in close proximity to the person. But, I've found the very same is true of a square, rectangular, or some other not-so-accurately measured shape of corral. A horse will round out the corners in these not-round pens and they can work just as well as a round one.

Let's take one type of very common round pen work that provides a discernable example of the two approaches I am addressing. In videos, demos, clinics, and such where a horse is worked at liberty in a round pen, one of the most common things presented is a person in the middle of the pen with a horse running circles out by the panels. In this scenario, it often can be observed that the person is actively driving the horse around the pen. Then, the person lets off that pressure, steps back, and sucks the horse into a vacuum close to the person.

It's a trick that typically works, and works fast. Many a person has wowwed an audience with this maneuver, and I remember thinking how amazing this kind of thing seemed when I started out. I even did it some myself. But, this example doesn't represent what I am looking for in horsemanship these days. That is because of the reason behind why this method works and how the horse feels about being in this situation.

If a person sends a horse out on the rail to go, run, and be driven, the person makes it pretty miserable for the horse. Then when the person backs off the pressure, it sucks the horse in, but not because it feels good to be with the person, but rather because it feels so bad to be out there in flee mode running around. And, it's not lost on the horse that the person is the reason behind the ill feeling of being made to go run around the pen.

Plus, when we drive horses into circling us in a round pen we are encouraging them to get away from us. If we stop and think about this we can realize that we don't ever want our horses to feel like they need to get away from us. Surely we seek the opposite result and desire that our horses have no better place in the world than being right there with us. Yet I see this kind of round pen work demonstrated over and over again. Often with the horse approaching the person with ears penned and tail swishing, feeling all pinched up inside. But because a person got a clearly bothered, untethered horse to come and stand by him in a round pen in two minutes, it's thought to be quite wonderful and an example of skilled horsemanship.

Rather than setting it up so that running out there on the rail stinks, and coming to the person stinks, too, just a little less, there are alternatives. The round pen can be used as a means to allow the horse to search out for himself that things truly can be better with the person. This helps to build with-you-ness (as Harry would say) between the horse and person. The hope, then, is that this work helps to build a foundation that can carry good feelings and togetherness into other areas we'd like to go to with our horses.

As with the above driving-the-horse scenario, the next example of round pen work involves a horse running around the pen out by the panels with a person in the center. This certainly looks similar to what was happening in the previous example. The difference is that in our new example the person is not doing anything to make the horse run around. Quite the contrary.

If I'm the person in the pen in this example, I'll be working to get the horse's attention. I want to help him come to his own decision to stop running and think about coming to me rather than forcing it happen. I do this by standing quietly in the center at first to see if by chance the horse will acknowledge me.

If the horse doesn't seem to take notice of me, then I will do something to interrupt his outward directed busy-ness. That something is often smacking my chap with the end of a lead rope to make a loud noise or whacking a flag on the ground. I will try to gauge this kind of overture to be big enough to be effective but not so big as to make things terribly worse. A dull horse might take a pretty big gesture, and a sensitive horse might take the slightest nudging. And I would probably try doing whatever I do only once at first to see what happens. It is a way to say, "Hey horse...I'm standing over here in the pen with you. Why don't you quit all the running around, come over here, and try relaxing a bit?"

When a horse is troubled in a round pen and running along the panels, or perhaps even going back and forth by the gate or the side of the pen closest to the barn or his buddies, I learned from Harry to think of this as a horse's thought being outside of the pen. The horse wants to escape the confines of the pen, and you can almost see that the horse's brain has popped out of his head and bounced outside of the panels. His feet and physique are working hard to get his body over to where his brain is. So, when I make a kerwhack of some kind there in the middle of the round pen, this interrupts his thought of working hard to get out of the pen.

A good kerwhack often will stop a horse's agitated fluster—at least for a moment. It becomes suddenly vitally important that he check out what is going on with the idiot in the middle of the pen. To accomplish this, the horse's brain needs to be recalled from over yonder and pop back into his head. And... it draws his attention to the person. Sometimes this will be the first break in the running around, and things can start to change for the better with the horse.

But, there are occasions when the horse may speed up and go harder at the first kerwhack or two. That harkens back to the first example. One may think they have witnessed me driving the horse around the pen, but that isn't what happened. Yes, I got active and the horse squirted harder around the pen. But, a kerwhack that is not directed at the horse is not the same in presentation as when a person drives a horse. One is done with intent at the horse, the other is not. A horse definitely senses the difference.

Eventually, even a horse intent on running away begins to look me up more and more. Almost always when given time and well-timed kerwhacks a horse will end up making the choice to try coming in close to me and standing. I'll be the first to admit that this process takes longer than driving a horse to misery and then sucking him in. The results, however, are profoundly different and worth every effort.

To see a horse begin to search for something new in the round pen because I intervened in his dilemma is a thrill. One can watch the wheels turn in his mind as he considers stopping, turning, facing me, and coming in close. And when a horse finally decides on his own to try coming to the middle of the pen to check me out and softens as I pet him when he does...there's nothing else like it. It is a singularly happy moment because it is not "mechanical," but rather results from establishing a positive relationship.

Once a horse begins to draw to and feel good about being with a person, the stage is set to begin directing the horse to try other things. Offer a feel, for instance, to see if the horse can take a couple of steps out around you close and then come back. Sometimes a horse remains dubious and needs to go out to the panels and run around some more. So what. Just let him go experience it. Remain the sweet spot in the pen and intervene enough to get him finding you again. He will work out for himself that running out there with his mind outside the pen doesn't feel nearly as good as being relaxed and still in the middle close to you.

The round pen certainly can be a helpful tool for setting up a good relationship with a horse. Rather than using it as a tool for forcing a horse to choose between a rock and a hard place, use it to allow a horse to search and feel like he came to his own conclusions, solved his own problems, and found a good friend right there close by.

Tack and Gear

Mirage and me in a decent snow here in Virginia. Mirage is decked out in a side pull with split reins and my treeless saddle all made by Jamey Wilcox [www.sjsaddleryinc.com]. (Photo: Carol Moates)

A horse owner contacted me recently to see about getting some help with her horse. As the conversation reached the point of scheduling me to come out, she asked a curious question:

"I don't have a round pen yet, but can we still work on some things?"

A handful of clients have asked this same question over the years. It got me thinking about how it can be easy to focus too much on tack and gear...even excellent, potentially helpful tack and gear.

When I began my horsemanship journey years ago I obsessively sought good information on getting better with horses. I attended all the clinics I could, watched every video I could get my hands on, and read books and magazines by the boxful. But in the beginning it was not easy to recognize the nuances of the horse work being done by the horse folks I hoped to learn from. The stuff being used by them, however, was obvious to see. Right away I noticed that some gear in particular was employed by a large percentage of these clinicians. It was easy to get the impression that there might be some essential relationship between good horsemanship and those things in particular.

Wade tree saddles, round pens, rope halters, macate reins, hackamores, and flags stood out to me. In other disciplines I might as easily have cued into lunge tapes, dressage whips, any number of bits/bridles, and so on. To confuse matters all the more, some of the horsemanship teachers I ran across even openly stressed particular types of gear or tack as being central to success.

My first experiences with horsemanship clinician Harry Whitney proved to be the point at which I fully understood that there is no magic in the gear. I attended two consecutive weeks of his clinics at his place in Arizona. I wrote honestly about the experience in the book *A Horse's Thought* saying:

"Hanging between two reins is a thought,' I heard Harry Whitney say.
The statement proved profound for me. Profound in its

truth and simplicity. It pretty much wrecked everything I'd been working on for a couple of years with horses."

Part of the seismic shift in horsemanship understanding I experienced when watching Harry work horses on that trip was that good horsemanship is not about the gear. Unlike so many of the previous clinics and videos I had seen where the gear used was rather homogeneous (everyone arrived with the same kind of rope halter, for instance), horse owners handed Harry horses with web halters, leather halters, and rope halters. Harry never batted an eye; he just took the lead ropes and went to work. I even watched him get stunning results in groundwork using only a lariat around horses' necks, getting the same nice changes in those horses as he had with those in halters.

I watched him ride in treeless saddles, roping saddles, trail saddles, and dressage saddles. In fact, I even observed Harry demonstrate that getting a horse more "with you" is not about a particular kind of gear by simply taking hold of a horse's bottom lip. Within a couple of minutes, he had that horse leading willingly just by offering a feel on the lip-hold using no gear whatever.

I began to understand that getting better with horses is about noticing where horses' minds are focused. It is about getting those horses' thoughts to shift to be with us, and thus convince them to be willing partners regardless of what tools are available.

Back to my recent client experience...I answered her, "No, we don't need a round pen. We can get working with whatever you have there."

It ended up that she didn't have anything in the way of a corral. We worked out in an open pasture with a halter and lead rope, found plenty to work on, and got some nice changes going between her and her horse.

Now don't get me wrong. This discussion isn't to say that having some nice gear is a bad thing. For the record, for

Harry Whitney works a horse in a rope halter with a flag in the round pen at his place in Salome, Arizona.

instance, I have a round pen. It is a great tool, especially for allowing a horse the freedom to move at liberty while remaining close to a person. But, a small square or rectangular pen works the same, the horse just rounds out the corners. Or as mentioned above, one can get plenty done without a corral just using a halter and lead rope, or lariat if that's what is on hand. Even the tight confines of a stall still allow room enough to get helpful horsemanship work accomplished.

And yet, there are times when a round pen is the cat's pajamas for helping a horse in some ways; it's just not essential to progress. All this is true because the positive changes brought about in a horse through our horsemanship take place within the horse's mind. The tools we use are most effective when used in a way to help a horse to think along with us and become a relaxed and willing partner rather than just used as a means to get mechanical reactions from the horse. And when the *relationship*

Before I put a halter on this young colt, I am using a lariat to begin working with him. I am looking for him to recognize a feel and search out where to be in relation to me and the rope. (Photo: Janet Doyle)

between a person and a horse truly improves, that shift can show beneficial effects in many areas.

An example of this would be discovering that achieving some improvements in the groundwork with a horse also produced improvements in the riding. When the understanding between the person and horse begins to improve, relaxation begins to show up where before there was tension. Willingness can develop in the horse where there was none before, and undesirable symptoms sometimes will evaporate without working on them specifically.

Certainly, some types of gear may fit a person better than others, and thereby benefit the work being attempted. For instance, I find the type of lead rope that is made from a particular kind of plastic that is light as a feather horrible. It does not pass along the feel a person presents on the line as well as a heavier piece of tree line or yacht rope. But, that does not mean they will not work if your presentation is right.

I keep a flag on hand as I find it to be a very helpful horsemanship tool at times. My favorite flag is a decapitated golf club with streamers cut from a feed bag taped to the end. I've used a bunch of different types of flags over the years—every kind of home brewed variety right on up to some rather pricey professionally produced ones—and if I pick the right golf club to take the hacksaw to, my preferred style has the best combination of lightness, length, and streamer action for me. And catch the right yard sale or thrift store, and the flag costs only about a dollar to make.

Affordability aside, it is the flag itself I prefer. There are clinicians I've seen who like a car antenna for a flag. Some prefer a solid square of cloth tied at a corner rather than streamers on the end. I've even seen a clinician with a flag cleverly constructed from a retractable fishing rod that folded up and fit in a back pocket when not in use. All such variations are personal preferences, but none are deal breakers when it comes to horse work. It's the timing and presentation when using the aids that matters.

And there are times where a particular type of gear can

I am riding Mirage in a rope halter with the lead rope tied back like reins. It may not be a proper side pull or bridle but works fine when the rider has the reins working to communicate with the horse.

be very helpful in specific situations. I pack around a leather side pull with reins, for instance. More than once I have come across a horse who is very resistant to the reins when being ridden in a bridle and bit, but put the side pull on and some of that resistance instantly disappears. Most likely, the bit is a cue that relates to past experiences and intensifies ill feelings in these horses. Head gear with reins but no bit seems to help get some of that baggage out of the way. But again, it's not essential to have a side pull and the same work can be done with the bit.

The point is that while particular gear can be helpful, or fit one's sensibilities better than other kinds, the gear itself always is secondary to how it is used with a horse. And, there is no magic in the gear. The magic is in the horsemanship skills that a person acquires. The mark of the consummate horse person is in the kind of relationship that she or he is able to establish with a horse using whatever is available—perhaps even when no gear is available. Feel, timing, balance, presentation...such things outweigh tack and gear every time.

Which leads me to one last thought related to the subject: that different horses will present us with very different challenges, so there is no cookie cutter approach to horsemanship in general that will work for all of them.

Yes, there are some fundamentals. A big one being that if your horse's mind is not centered with you, then you are going to be hard-pressed to make a meaningful change in that horse. But, where one horse at a given point might benefit most from being worked loose in a round pen, another might best be worked on line. One horse might be mentally stuck and need to be encouraged to have a forward thought to go where another might need to be slowed down from blasting off.

Being too focused on a specific method related to a particular piece of gear may mean you miss excellent opportunities for helping a horse. It's better to keep all the available options open and use some ingenuity with the skills in that horsemanship toolbox, and not depend overly on the tools themselves.

Trailer Loading

Leo, owned by Bruce Evans, provides a good example of a horse who is not thinking into a trailer shown in part by his sideways stance and ears directed backwards. (Photo: Bruce Evans)

Trailer loading projects frequently come up in the horsemanship clinics and lessons that I teach. It's no surprise. Perhaps the real surprise is that horses, with all that innate desire to have a good view of the landscape to see predators at a distance and the open space to flee at top speed, would ever get into a tiny metal box in the first place—for any reason.

Even with horses' hard-wired apprehension of tight spots, many do become easy to load, and some get good at it even after being tough loaders in the past. I really enjoy getting the chance to work on trailer loading with students. Asking a horse to think inside a trailer is a very observable means of getting a person to understand what it looks like to direct horses' thoughts. Gaining awareness of where a horse is thinking, and helping a horse to let go of thoughts other than the ones that lead to the goals that we seek (like getting into a trailer), is key to good horsemanship, and successful trailer loading.

Reflecting on past trailer loading sessions with students, the first thing that comes to mind is that some of the troubles I've witnessed weren't really trailer loading troubles per se. For example, I had a client with a horse she couldn't load. She said that even looking at the trailer would cause this big, 17 hand gelding to rip the lead rope from the handler's hands and go tearing off into the distance.

I arrived at the farm to see a pick-up and trailer positioned in a spacious parking lot ready for a horse. The gooseneck trailer sported two straight-load spots behind a tack room with a ramp that lowered for horse access. To begin, I asked the owner to show me how things went when she tried to load the horse.

She disappeared into the barn and brought the tall, solid chestnut gelding out on a halter and lead rope. She led the horse towards the trailer. As they got close, the gelding's head went up and he began looking around. She made a bee line for the open end of the trailer, went up the ramp, and in ahead of the horse. It looked like she might succeed in getting the big fella to load, but then he balked at the top of the ramp. She tightened her grip and shortened up on the lead rope, and in a flash she was back out on the ramp wrestling with the horse. The gelding threw his shoulder into her, and she made an effort to hold her position, but the horse reared up, spun past her, ripped the lead rope out of her hands, took off at a high rate of speed, and disappeared back into the barn.

"I see," I said.

I walked towards the barn to fetch the horse. Someone had caught the gelding and came out of the barn leading the him.

"Thanks," I said taking the rope.

I led the horse over towards the trailer but stopped about 50 feet short of it in a nice open spot. I asked the horse to back up by presenting a feel with a bit of an up and down shake on the lead rope. The horse was jazzed up, head high, and looking all over the place. The gelding took a rather mechanical step back and I released the ask. Then I slapped my shotgun chaps with the end of the lead rope to make a loud POP!

The horse did a double take and focused right on me for a second, then he went back to doodling around. I made another slap, and when his gaze snapped onto me this time I asked him to back up a couple of steps, and he did, relaxing a bit and letting go of the other thoughts racing in his brain.

I reached over and stroked him once on the nose. He softened a bit more. I asked him to step his front end over to my right and then go around me a half circle. I changed hands on the lead rope and had him step his front end back past me over to my left and then go and circle me in the other direction. I asked him to halt without turning in to face me, and he did. Then I backed him up again, and so on.

The horse, after becoming mentally centered on me with the chap slapping and a little groundwork, followed along rather nicely with what I presented because he had let go of his busy-brained bouncing around that was presenting before. The groundwork lasted maybe four minutes. Then I walked over to

Sometimes getting a horse to load willingly is helped or even solved by getting the horse with you mentally by doing some ground work before approaching the trailer. Here, I have Jubal, a client's horse, thinking along with me and following a feel—an excellent precursors to a favorable loading experience. (Photo: Janet Doyle)

the back of the trailer, stood on the ground off to the left side, and with my left hand holding the lead rope I asked the horse to step up the ramp into the trailer on the driver's side compartment. He went right up in it and stood still, relaxed.

Now, this is a particularly dangerous spot for a horseman to be in—not because of the horse, who was doing great, but because of the horse owner who was ready to kill me! After who-knows-how-many hours of fighting with a horse who won't load, when someone comes in, grabs the lead rope, does a little groundwork away from the trailer, and up the horse goes into the trailer and stands lickety-split...you can see why one might be in danger of bodily harm. But the point here is that the trailer was never the real issue with this horse—he wasn't particularly scared of it or traumatized by trying to get into it. The issue was that the owner did not have the horse's mind centered and steadied where it was available to be directed.

The job that day really ended up being to help the owner to see when her horse was not with her mentally. And to recognize that condition if it happened at any point from the moment she went to the stall and haltered the horse. I coached her through some groundwork and pointed out how the horse looked when he was not centered up with her mentally (head up, looking all over the place, muscles tight, legs dancing a jig, ears sideways and back, etc). When she was able to get him more with her by getting big enough to gain his full attention, he relaxed some and he loaded just fine for her, too.

But, not all trailer loading work is so simple as the above example turned out to be. This gets back to the trailer being a great visual for seeing if a horse's thought is directed where the human wants it to be or not. Part of the key here is that when a horse thinks about going someplace (like into a trailer), he then can take himself there not only without a fight, but with a willingness. That is what we hope capable horsemanship can provide us humans, the ability to suggest lightly to our horses that they undertake some task and that they be relaxed and willing to do it.

I was called out by a client to load a mare who needed to be trailered to be bred. This horse had grown up on the farm where she lived and had never been in a trailer before. The mare was around seven years old. When I arrived and met the mare, I put my rope halter on her and did some ground work. She clearly knew nothing about following a feel presented by a person. The owner was not around, but the breeder who had hired me to get her loaded was there and had brought a goose-neck stock trailer. I was pleased with that option; when loading a horse who has not been in a trailer before, getting a trailer with plenty of space and open slats along the top of the sides can be way easier to work with than trying to get one to go into smaller, more enclosed types.

The dog days of summer were upon us in Virginia and it was hitting 100 degrees with plenty of humidity in the afternoons. The trailer was parked inside the gate of a pasture and backed up against a little incline to make the step up into the back of the trailer as short as possible. The rear end of the trailer opened up fully, and the rear gate swung to the passenger's side and stayed open on its own up against some brush. A grassy area on a slight slope stretched out behind the trailer providing plenty of room to work in.

With my flag—a decapitated golf club with feed sack streamers taped to it—I began doing a little ground work out behind the trailer. Once I had her used to the flag and more mentally centered with me, I stepped to the driver's side at the back of the open trailer and with the lead rope in my left hand I put a feel on the rope and asked her to look up into it. She shuffled this way and that, head and gaze here and there, and she wasn't about to follow my suggestion to even check out the inside of the metal box. This is where a good trailer loading shines as a teaching tool—it is very obvious to see when a horse does not want to think inside a trailer.

As I offered that she think inside, I began to flag and kept up some flagging until she began to let go of thinking about the other things around the pasture and began to think into the

At one of my clinics, this horse showed up late when the owners had extreme difficulty getting her into the trailer. I am directing the horse to think into the trailer—and I worked on this with her during several short sessions each day over a few days of the clinic. By the third session, she made the choice to walk up into the trailer. By the end of the clinic, she was loading quite willingly.

open trailer. When she did, I quit flagging as a release and tried to present a "sweet spot" to her. Sometimes, she would start to take an interest inside the trailer, which was easy to see as she lowered her head and looked up in there. At other times, she would hold out big-time. That kept me flagging my arm off looking for a change, often with the horse even backing up away from the trailer quite a ways. Eventually, she even reared, spun, and ripped the lead rope from my hands and galloped away to the other side of the barn up the hill. Off I went to collect her and lead her back to the trailer for another try.

This scenario repeated over and over again, and she got

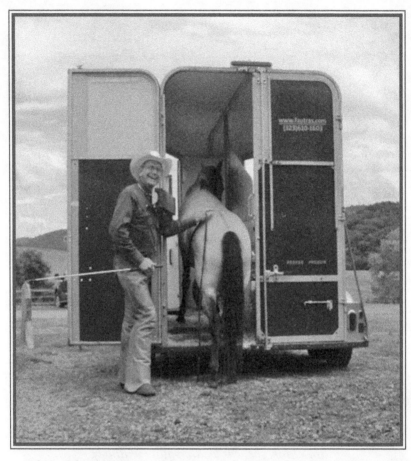

After making progress with getting a horse to choose to go part way into a trailer willingly, clinician Harry Whitney provides a nice, relaxed moment for the progress to work out really well for the horse.

away from me a few times in the process. It probably went on for an hour before I got her to take a really good, long look inside the open trailer. At one point, she even tried going around the trailer gate into the thick bushes to evade going inside the metal box. I will hand it to her, she *was* searching when I asked her to let go of other things and search for what I was asking for, but she showed *way* more creativity than the average equine for coming up with other options!

As the heat soared, we both became soaked with sweat and I noticed the mare begin to look more regularly inside the trailer when I asked her to. I stepped up into the trailer, made some noise kicking on the sides and the floor to get her used to the sounds, and then offered for her to come forward inside with me. She seemed determined not to put entering that trailer onto her menu of options. I've seen very few horses hold out as long and strongly as she did before at least trying to put a foot on the trailer floor.

But I knew eventually she'd start to mark off her list more of the things that she was trying that weren't working out so well (thanks to the flagging) and come around to trying what I was suggesting. I persisted, matter-of-factly, and just kept presenting what I was after over and over and over. To make a three hour long story shorter, eventually she put a foot up on the trailer floor and I quickly released my asking and rubbed her sweetly for that. Eventually, she tried putting both front feet in the trailer. Then we hit another plateau. But even with two feet inside the trailer, sometimes her mind was back outside. I continued to handle the situation as I had all along, flagging when she was regressing to thinking around outside or when she was stuck and not progressing forwards. I was careful to release for her inching in the direction of what I was looking for, and I hoped to get her to search and choose to come further inside.

The marathon loading session ended all of a sudden. She got her body straight as in arrow to the trailer, looked way up in it past me, pointed her ears both fully forward, and when I asked her to step inside, she did...willingly, all the way in and just stood there. When she finally put the option of getting into that metal box on the menu options and did it, she applied herself 100 percent to the choice. The change was amazing and wonderful.

The thing about this kind of progress is that by taking the time to allow the horse to search (even when it may seem like you may never get there), when the horse comes around to trying what you'd like her to do, the horse feels like it was her decision. I didn't box her in and drive her into the trailer. I didn't get a group of guys to put ropes behind her and throw her in there. I just out-persisted her, asking for her to load and making all those other ideas not work out so well. And she got the chance to go through all her range of things she'd rather do first besides getting in that trailer until finally she said, "Okay...I guess maybe I'll try getting in the trailer and perhaps then this idiot with the flag will quit!"

Bingo!

I hung out with her in the trailer and petted on her for a couple of minutes trying to make that the best place she'd ever experienced. Then before she got any other ideas, I backed her off the trailer and out about 15 feet into the grassy spot. We stood there and I rubbed on her a minute. Then I brought her forward, stood off to the side, and asked her to load. She walked right up into the trailer again, and I gave her some much appreciated rest there in the shade before backing her out. We repeated the loading and resting a few more times, then I closed the door with her standing quietly inside and the driver hauled her on down the road.

I didn't hear more about that mare for a long time, but when the breeder eventually called me to help with another horse project I asked how the mare had gotten along. She said that the horse's ownership had come into dispute between different parties and the mare had loaded with no problem when one of the parties had showed up one night and stolen her.

Then, the actual owner had gone (unannounced) and gotten her back, and she loaded fine for him, too. And that every time since that long, hot summer afternoon we spent together, that horse just willingly has walked right up into any trailer slick as you please. So it seems those three hours of work changed the mare from one of the hardest to load to an easy loader, hopefully for life.

Trailer loading is a subject that lends itself to all kinds of horsemanship insights, and here I've just touched on a couple examples to make one major point—that horses' minds are the key to our relationships with them, and that this can be quite ob-

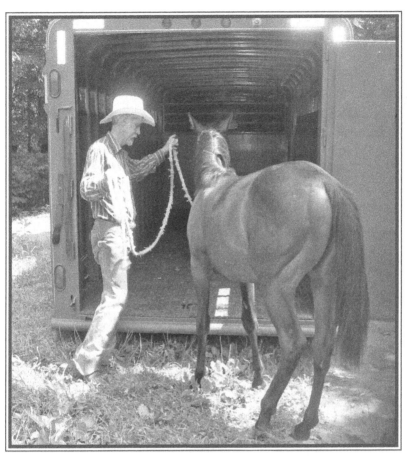

I am giving my mare Mirage a chance to think up into an open stock trailer during her first trailer loading experience. Here, she is not real straight, her ears aren't forward, and she is not thinking strongly into the trailer. I would get quiet and offer a sweet spot between us when she checked out the inside of the trailer. When she started to back away or otherwise think outside of the box, I would get a little busy, clucking and perhaps even slapping my chaps with the end of the lead rope to try and redirect her thoughts back inside the trailer. Within a short time, she got very straight to the trailer, her ears went forward, and she chose to step her front feet inside. The hind feet followed soon after and she's been an easy loader ever since. (Photo: Carol Moates)

servable when we go to load them into a trailer. Trailer loading, and other "jobs" we do with our horses are opportunities to see where we may lack in our communication with our horses. Such tasks may not always be fun to deal with, but if we use them to see when our horses are thinking along with us or not and figure out good ways to get them to think along with us, then they can be the ultimate teaching experiences.

The Big Stick

Niji and me during a photo shoot to promote the release of one of the **Six Colts, Two Weeks** *books.* *(Photo: Carol Moates)*

Preface

Here's a rarity! A previously unpublished chapter/essay from the vault. This chapter was written in 2008; at the time I had just wrapped up *A Horse's Thought* and had begun working on the book *Between the Reins*. I'm not entirely sure why it didn't make it into *Between the Reins*, or one of the later titles in the five-book Honest Horsemanship series, but it has sat collecting dust on a hard drive for more than a decade until I came across it this morning.

I think the reason that I never published this chapter is that I realized, even early on, that there are other things afoot in the moment described in it besides what my more narrow understanding at that point could comprehend. Today, I would be much better equipped to see where Niji's mind left the scene earlier and to deal with it before having a huge issue to deal with. I still was missing so much back then, not that Niji ever made it easy! And I sure learned a ton from that sorrel gelding.

But I want to share this chapter now because it opens a window into a time early in my horsemanship journey when I was really trying to improve, and experiencing really trying times at times. I know for certain that anyone who sets out on a horsemanship journey will experience the kind of circumstances and frustrations that I recorded in this bit of writing. It takes me back, and I have enjoyed sharing the truth of my experience with you readers all along the way.

I hope you enjoy reading this time-capsule from my horsemanship past as much as I appreciated finding it and reflecting on Niji and the hardships and triumphs that have gone into getting me to where I am today, even as I struggle with different challenges and enjoy new successes with horses all the time!

Whisper if You Want...I Carry a Big Stick!

That was IT! The end of the rope. I decided right then to walk that horse home, pull the saddle, maybe throw it across the yard for good measure, and put Niji back in his paddock... forever!

I was furious! Seemingly once and for all totally over-whelmed. I'm typically a fairly cool cucumber, especially around horses. In that moment, however, I was so angry I retreated to the end of the twenty foot lead rope—as far away from the sorrel gelding as that instant allowed—and imploded.

It was the farthest down the horsemanship toilet I'd ever been flushed. And it only took six years of all-out hard work to get that lousy with horses.

I struggled to gather any microscopic trace of reason remaining to calm my unhinged mind, but the frustration boiled over spilling out of my wrenched soul in idiotic shouts, stomps, and flailings of the arm not attached to the lead rope, like a broken windmill (yes...much like a 2 year old; glad I live in the middle of nowhere; let's keep this confession between us, shall we?).

In the flash of a second while riding the gelding, Niji had gotten head-strong and pulled around against my request to stay straight and continue on the road. I held my request on the rein, not pulling against him, just holding until he hopefully got the idea and then a release. Instead we ended up off the road, down a hill, into the trees, and backwards in our relationship to a place I prayed I'd never see again.

It was not a spook, or a buck, or a run-off, or even partic-ularly dangerous. To the onlooker it might have seemed funny, or ridiculous, or just a moment of temporary insanity ending in a circle back onto the farm road. In truth, however, it was a complete collapse of everything I had worked so hard and long to build up and get past with him.

Niji looking so innocent!

The trouble crescendoed. That's when I dismounted and lost my mind.

Two years I spent (no exaggeration) off-and-on working on this particular problem. The previous three months, I rode daily with the most excellent results. The problem even faded to little more than a distant memory. Then, to fall apart again in one terrible flash...it was, quite simply, more than I could take.

Niji kept tension on the rope, backing away, wide-eyed wondering what the heck was my problem? (Like he didn't know! Looking so innocent.) If a tree had been any closer I would have beat my head against it, since I hadn't tried that yet.

The truth is that Niji didn't know. I'll grant him that. But when you work so hard and get through a sticky point with a horse, and then it returns worse than ever, it feels like the horse is just in-your-face choosing to defy you. This is the perfect example. We clearly worked through the head-strong problem. It disappeared completely for weeks—on exactly the same road, in exactly the same tack, with me offering exactly the same cues as now proved ineffective. It took near super-human effort to remind myself that it's not defiance, that there are real reasons for the trouble. And that I just stink as a horseman.

Well, that's the way I felt about it at the time, anyhow. But, this is a story of redemption. It's a recounting of how horse difficulties can seem overwhelming to the point that your horsemanship toolbox seems completely exhausted: turned up-side-down, spilled out, and even shook hard to be sure nothing is stuck in there somewhere to try. Yet, by looking at the pile of past horsemanship experiences scattered on the ground at your feet for the ten thousandth time, you still can find the seeds of a new approach. An innovative slant to break the chain of trouble can catapult one from the toilet to the treetops. I was shocked at the about-face that happened two minutes after my meltdown with Niji. It simply remains one of the best examples of how a single tiny thread remained to pull me out of an equine abyss. The thinnest hair of help trailed back to an obscure memory of clinician Harry Whitney working at a clinic that ultimately got me thinking my way out of such a terrible downward spiral.

To make an incredibly long story short, the history of Niji's head-strong deal leads back to the first time I began to ride him daily to feed the other horses two years earlier. That trek is a couple miles round-trip. One leg of the journey leads along a tight right of way, about 12 feet wide, defined by barbed wire fences on either side that ends at the bottom of a steep hill at a gate. We rode this route for three days with no problems. Then, returning on the fourth day, out of the blue, Niji refused to leave that gate and go up the hill. I exhausted every bit of pressure-and-release I could think of from the saddle to persuade him otherwise. Two horrendous afternoons trying to work it out ended in my retreat from that area altogether. This head-strong behavior then spilled over into other areas where it hadn't been before. Even at the home paddock I suddenly had a full blown problem on my hands.

I worked with the gelding over many months with some good progress on the problem. It never cleared out completely, though. Finally, for circumstances beyond my control, riding ceased here for many months. Niji got an unexpected vacation, and so did I.

After the long sabbatical, I started again with Niji. I decided to start from the ground up to see if we could just dissolve the past problem with a re-start. Things went fantastic on the ground. I realized in retrospect, though, that the trouble never presented much in the ground work. Climbing into the saddle, things started out well riding him just around the paddock. Soon, to my dismay, the head-strong tendency reappeared. I committed to putting 90 days on him to see if dedication and consistency would overcome the issue.

By 60 days, we were back to roving the farm. My pressure and release experiments in general cleared out the problem, and we got on then without residual trouble of that head-strong defiance. I started riding him again to feed the other horses, going half the distance as before since no horses were in the far pasture beyond the gate of my nightmares where Niji's trouble began. Life was great for three weeks! And then....

There I was losing my mind, leading Niji just after the head-strong issue returned that miserable day. What triggered it I guess I will never know. It just suddenly started as mysteriously as the first time.

Then, in a flash, two quick thoughts crossed my brain—

Niji and me riding along the farm road. This ride was much later and produced much better results than the time recounted in this chapter. (Photo: Carol Moates)

first that I'd like to whack that horse with a big stick! (just an evil fantasy, of course)—which made me remember Harry using a flag from the saddle in the round pen one day. He reached out by the eye of a sticky, head-strong horse to turn him with the flag. It wasn't simply a mechanical turning of a horse, though. In Harry speak, it was to, "block a thought." The horse he rode was "committed to" going straight when Harry wanted to turn. The flagging worked by providing another means other than reins or legs to help block the horse's idea of going straight like it wanted to, and come back to following his rider's lead. I wondered if that would work here?

There were sticks everywhere, so I got a nice one that was flag-like in length and feel. I mounted up and rode Niji down the road about five steps, and there we went, headed off the road to the left. As best I could, I worked rein and leg to adjust back, still giving him that chance first. As expected, he plowed right through my suggestion. So I stuck the stick out there into his field of vision. He stopped with a, "What's that?" surprise. Then plowed onwards with his agenda anyway.

I held rein and leg and then shook the stick more, even tapping his jaw finally, and that horse reacted then and came right back to the road. I immediately dropped the stick from sight and went to a complete release as he walked nice and straight. Five steps later, he tried it again. Again I went through the same process in quick succession. Again the stick worked almost instantly. I am not lying when I say two minutes of flagging with that big stick was all it took to fix the trouble that had me so desperately overwhelmed for so long. At that point, the stick no longer even was needed the rest of the way home, and the ride was a joy.

I was overjoyed. Past experiences with Niji proved that once this problem starts, I'm doomed to weeks of regression with him. That's why I was so distressed. This result was a miracle. I just couldn't believe it.

Afterwards, two big points stuck with me. First, Niji quickly stopped being head-strong in all situations except one:

where he sometimes (not always) sees other horses close by and wants to go to them. That remains a place where this problem persists, so the stick wasn't a silver bullet completely clearing out all the troubles. However, there were profound changes immediately upon using the stick as a tool to break the terrible cycle we found ourselves in, over and over, for a very long time.

I am left reassured that new possibilities for getting beyond a problem with a horse are always at our fingertips if we just stop and see them. Experiences hopefully collect in our horsemanship lives that lead us to figure out possibilities that work towards clearing out troubles with our horses. Nothing fills our horsemanship toolbox with new tools like getting out and working with our horses, using some imagination, and surviving the lousy times. If I had thought about Harry using the flag to help block horses' thoughts from the saddle to get them to a better place inside before (note that Niji was leaving the road not because he was relaxed and felt like a stroll, but because he was bothered inside causing him to forcibly turn and disregard my direction in a worried way), and used a flag to fix the problem at the very beginning of the original trouble two years earlier, it likely never would have grown to the monster it did. But, I plan to learn from my mistakes, and I won't be putting Niji away into a paddock for life.

The other thing that nagged me about this whole trouble was how different Niji reacted when I was on the ground versus when I was mounted. Every single time his turning problem occurred, if I dismounted and took the lead rope, the gelding not only improved, but never fought against me. That "defiance" was saddle specific.

I asked Harry about this. He said that horses are usually quite willing to follow a strong leader, either within a herd of horses or with a human. But, the experience is always following another being that is on the ground and is clearly seen as a separate entity with body language at work. Some horses just don't make the connection at first between the person on the ground calling the shots, and that same person who largely disappears from view onto the horse's back where instructions are felt only and not really visual.

I was amazed that if I stood on the ground, even during an episode of trouble, and worked the reins giving the same exact cues I would from the saddle, Niji responded perfectly. But, the second I stepped up into the saddle and used those very same cues, I had absolutely no luck. Flagging from the saddle helped to put more of me into that outer, visual world than I ever could with just reins and legs.

This is a fundamental difference in understanding and key to why people think a horse is just insubordinate when, in truth, he's just being a horse. So, whisper if you want to, but from now on I'm carrying a big stick!

Haltering

Relaxed and mentally present, Festus cooperates as I remove his halter before putting on his bridle. (Photo: Carol Moates)

Haltering or bridling a horse is an often overlooked, quite important, and very telling aspect of the relationship between a person and a horse.

Horses are always on. By this I mean that our equine companions are learning about and reassessing their relationships to us humans continually, moment by moment, with each interaction. We humans tend to gloss over some areas when interacting with horses, not considering those moments to be important or really thinking much about them.

But to horses, all interactions between them and us have significance. What we do in each instant that we spend with them comes to bear measurably on their relationships with us. One place where humans often gloss over what's really taking

Harry Whitney and Peacham, a gelding owned by Sarah Barron. Harry presents himself carrying a bridle to the horse at Mendin' Fences Farm in Rogersville, Tennessee.

place in that relationship is in bridling and haltering.

Putting a halter or bridle on a horse may seem like no big deal when a horse stands fine for it. But, horses' reactions to the process can range from horses who simply stand to those who flee the scene and must be caught. Even if a horse stands okay for a person, it is not uncommon to see the horse glancing sideways wishing to escape or to see someone chasing a horse's head around trying with some difficulty to get the horse to be still enough to accept the headgear.

If you have a loose horse in a stall or a round pen, what chances do you think you have for that horse to just come over and put his nose into his head gear for you to buckle or tie it on him? Try it with a horse or two. What happens is telling of the relationship between that horse and humans.

I remember witnessing a session at a clinic years ago that I found astonishing and changed the nature of my thinking about haltering/bridling a horse. My horsemanship mentor Harry Whitney was helping someone who had a horse that wanted to squirm, not take a bit, and not be bridled. Harry pointed out how the horse was thinking hard away from the person in general when she went to bridle the horse. The horse had been led into a round pen on a halter and lead rope, but now the halter was off and tied around the horse's neck to clear the head for the bridle. Harry had the owner turn the horse loose in the round pen. Harry entered the pen and the owner handed him the bridle as she exited the pen with her halter and lead rope.

I watched Harry work on what unfolded next for a long time—it was at least an hour, and probably quite a bit more. He stood in the middle of the round pen and asked the horse to acknowledge him. The horse had other plans complete with other thoughts to tend to outside of the pen. Harry slapped his chaps with the reins. The horse stopped moving about and took notice of him. Harry waited. The horse soon went back to finding distractions, to which Harry made a little noise to draw the horse's mind back to him.

Over the course of time, the horse let go more and more

Harry presents Peacham the bridle and Peacham contemplates.

of the other things he wanted to use as distractions and came to rest his thoughts on Harry. When the horse was attentive to Harry, Harry got still and offered what I might call a real "sweet spot" for the horse. Certainly, this horse knew that Harry was holding the bridle for a reason, and what that meant. But increasingly, due to Harry's persistent interventions—and as the alternatives to coming to Harry to be bridled didn't work out so well—the horse became more and more willing to come and try being close to Harry. Focusing on Harry worked out better than anything else in that pen.

Finally, the horse came and stood close enough to Harry for him to reach up and pet the horse's the face. I thought, "Brilliant! He's got the horse there and now he can put the bridle on."

But that's not what Harry did.

With the same patience and attention to where the horse's thoughts were, Harry got really particular. Harry held the bridle out open in such a way that the horse could come to it and place his nose in the nose band. The horse did not do that, but the offer was clear to see.

As the horse would think about a wonderful distraction as an alternative to submitting to being bridled (sometimes just barely perceptible, like a slight shifting glance of the eyes to the side), Harry would make a little noise. The preceding work Harry had done to get the horse standing quietly beside him had established their relationship in such a way that the horse understood that some such action by Harry meant to bring his focus back to Harry and the task at hand.

The reluctance the horse had to putting his nose in the bridle remained palpable but Harry never forced it or even hurried the process. I sat there wondering if I would be able to be so patient? He just offered and waited, and didn't let any of the horse's side-tracking thoughts take root.

In an amazing moment for me, I witnessed this horse sigh, visibly relax by lowering his head and softening his muscles, and then lean towards Harry and voluntarily put his nose right in the nose band, quietly take the bit in his mouth, and wait there relaxed to be buckled up into his bridle.

I was stunned! I had never seen such a thing—that a horse could be communicated with in such a way as to really participate in being bridled or haltered. Not just stand still for it. Not just be okay with it. But actually show a willingness to *participate* in it.

Harry had not forced the horse to have the idea to stick his nose in the bridle, but rather had just made a whole round pen full of other options the horse tried first not work out so well. By not forcing the horse to be bridled and by not making the other destracty-things impossible, the horse had been allowed to make choices for himself, and he knew it. Harry's patient persistence had convinced the horse to keep searching for something along the way. And, when the horse found things that got him warmer to what Harry was looking for, Harry had helped those work out really well until finally, the horse was taking the bit and sticking his nose voluntarily into the nose band.

There is a lot in this example in terms of horsemanship to grasp, but regarding the haltering/bridling of horses, I've never viewed the task the same way since seeing this session. Knowing what can be between a person and a horse regarding the act of haltering/bridling set me on a course to try and achieve that level of willingness and participation from horses whenever I can.

Not every horse is going to come through to a willingness to being bridled or haltered the same way the one in this example did. But I think it is a good illustration to hold up to use as a benchmark to strive for.

If we neglect the chance to foster willingness and togetherness in what we tend to think of as "smaller" actions with our horses then we miss a great opportunity to build into those relationships as a whole the kind of mindfulness and partnership we seek in the "bigger" things. Everyone wants an attentive and willing horse when riding. We are on their backs—a rather vulnerable position to be in that makes humans perk up and pay attention to how their horses are feeling, responding, and performing. But letting things slide and not being particular

After some searching, Peacham willingly takes the bit.

in other areas with our horses, like in the haltering or bridling, means that we are giving the horse another message at those times; often that memo says: being attentive to us and engaged in what we are doing is not really very important.

Horses don't think as we do, "Oh, now we are riding, this is important so it is time to be attentive and behave." Horse have their self preservation wired quite close to the surface, and more so than humans often give them credit for. Horses pay attention to their environment keenly and constantly, and that includes scrutinizing everything that we humans do, whatever it may be, and whether we are riding or on the ground.

Standing to Mount

Harry Whitney stepping up into the saddle on a sturdy mule after a bit of ground work during a clinic in Salome, Arizona.

A horse not standing contentedly for a person to mount certainly is an inconvenience, and in some circumstances even dangerous. It is a fairly common problem, and one that comes up in my clinics and lessons often. So why do some horses jig around or walk off when it is time to be mounted, and what can be done to remedy the situation?

Reasons for this behavior can seem numerous: past bad experiences, ill fitting saddles, poor training, other horses or distractions nearby, and so on. But aside from a physical cause, like an ill fitting saddle or a sore back, the underlying root of the various other reasons is mainly that the horse's mind is not focused in the moment with the person. It sounds simple, and in a way it is, but it may not be obvious to a person until it is pointed out.

My horsemanship mentor, clinician Harry Whitney, is fond of saying, "When a horse's body and his mind are not in the same place at the same time, there's trouble in the household!" This certainly holds true in our instance here at the mounting block (or fence, or tailgate, or ground—wherever you want to mount from).

It is easy to visualize what a horse looks like who is having "trouble in the household." The horse may be moving about, showing some nervousness and tension with a head held high and wide eyed, perhaps even calling out with a shrill neigh.

Horses have primary thoughts. They also can have secondary, and probably tertiary thoughts, etc. But a horse almost always will fix his eyes on his primary thought, and that is the most important thing in his mind and in his environment at that moment. So, one big clue to look for with a horse who is jigging about at the mounting block is where his eyes are focused.

Often, a horse's gaze is focused out over yonder somewhere away from the person trying to mount. The horse has seized a diversion to try and mentally escape the scene even though his body is held there captive. This can be quite stressful to the horse. This scenario reminds me of an adult stepping between a youngster and his favorite TV show—the kid is going to work hard to look around you to keep up with what is taking place on TV rather than pay attention to you.

The interesting thing is that as badly as a horse may seem to want to be elsewhere, if a person does something in the immediate environment big enough to break the horse's thought away from over yonder and get it back here to where his body is, the horse often shows signs of settling and feeling better. The horse can start to settle and become more available to participate in the relationship with the person taking place there at the mounting block when he lets go of those side-tracking thoughts.

I often visualize the horse's brain having left his body and gone over the fence, down the hill, and to his buddies at the barn, for example. When I get "big enough" somehow to break through that distracted primary thought, the horse realizes there is something very important "back where his body is," so he really needs to have his brain there to take care of it. Thus, he recalls his brain, which leaves the barn, comes back up the hill, back over the fence, and into his head where he now has his primary thought back in the moment at the mounting block.

Some horses are more easily convinced to bring their focus back to the person and the task at hand than others. For a sensitive horse, it may only require a cluck or two, or a snap of the fingers. A horse more committed to diversions and duller to the handler may be persuaded to think back with a person only when something more dramatic is done. Flapping a training flag or slapping the end of a lead rope against the chaps are examples of this. In other words, not standing to be mounted (as with so many other horse behaviors we wish weren't presenting at times, like rushing off, crowding a person, etc.) can be a symptom of the underlying malady of a diverted mind.

Horses tend to have habits regarding their mental focus. If a horse is in the habit of leaving the scene mentally when it is time to do something with a person, then that is a situation that has been allowed to take place over time and become established. But, a person can tune into where a horse's thoughts are. Addressing distracted thoughts consistently so that the habit

After doing a little ground work from his perch, Harry asks a horse to step up along side him.

becomes a horse keeping focus on the person when something is going on between them can revolutionize the overall relationship for the better. If the rapport between a horse and a person is set up so that the horse expects that when the person asks something it is important enough to have his primary attention, then the horse is much more likely to be right there and relaxed for the handler when a request of any kind is made.

So, let's run through an example of how working on this might play out to provide a common scenario. Keep in mind that each horse and situation is different but, universally, until a

The horse is attentive to Harry now and fairly relaxed, and Harry is easily able to slide into the saddle onto a quiet horse who stands still.

horse brings his primary focus to a person, there is never really going to be a chance to have a fully willing partner in the situation.

In this example, we have a horse tacked up being led to the mounting block. Before the duo ever get there, the human pays attention to where the horse's mind is. The horse follows along calmly, head down, a step behind and not crowding the person, and there is no jigging about. If there is any indication that the horse isn't with the person mentally and following the feel presented as they go along, the person stops and addresses that with a little ground work. The person might back the horse, ask the horse to circle this way and that, and all the while getting big enough as necessary to make sure the horse's mind can let go of distractions to participate with the person on simple tasks.

The horse, now with the person, should fall into position again as the two walk along. There is a kind of sweet spot that can develop and is felt when things are right between a human and a horse. Even so, as one goes along one might test this to see that the horse is really mentally with the handler and not just going along on auto pilot. Do this, I might put a little feel on the reins or lead rope that the horse slow a little as we walk along. If he hears me and readily responds, great! Off we go. If not, I am going to address that his focus isn't fully on what we're doing.

By the time a person gets to the mounting block leading the horse this way, things should be flowing between them and any mental distractedness ought to be already addressed. Many times this approach eliminates the chance for mounting trouble ever to occur in the first place. I have worked with folks who had their mounting difficulties simply evaporate when the ground work in general began to address the horse's focus. We are concerning ourselves here with mounting troubles, but the truth is that the answer to a horse who has difficulty standing to be mounted is often the same as for the one who has trouble in other areas of interaction with humans, like being led or standing for the farrier—centering a distracted mind.

So, say I get to the mounting block after a good walk to it

from the pasture with a horse, but now the trouble still shows up. I step up there and ask the horse to sidle up alongside me and stand, but instead I have a horse who is prancing about. I will do the same thing I would do if this behavior had presented on the walk over—do a little ground work. This time I might direct from atop the mounting block, always focusing primarily on where my horse's primary thought is.

In this scenario, say the horse's head is high and turned away from me as he avoids coming in close along where I stand on the mounting block. I might slap my thigh with an open hand to get the horse's attention. This slap, or some similar attention getter, isn't done as a punishment or as a means to drive my horse in any way. It is, rather, an unemotional request that he look at me and get his brain on me and the mounting block where his body is.

When I get big enough to snap a horse's attention back to me, usually a horse will settle a bit and look at me. Once he is mentally present, I might ask him to step this way and that like I wound in any ground work. Once things are going well, I will send him off to one side or the other and then begin to bring him in straight, a step at a time, along in front of me and the mounting block. I like to put the hand not holding the reins or lead rope on the other side of the horse's neck to offer a little support and help steady his mind.

I take this sidling up beside me part slowly, a step at a time, being careful to be particular with the feel that I offer, offering releases and pauses for each correct step along the way so that the horse will know when he is getting the right answers to the asks that I present him. Often, when set up right, the horse makes it in the first try or two and stands there quietly. Sometimes, I can just get on at that point and that's it; the horse stands just fine. At other times, a horse may get immediately distracted again when I go to slide a leg over him—in which case I continue the work to keep the horse mentally present as I start to put my body into position to slide a leg over him. I may need to break this down into little pieces: leaning towards the horse, leaning over him, lifting my leg, etc.

If at first the horse remains distracted and unwilling to come in close and stand contentedly, I just send him out from the mounting block for a bit more ground work and try bringing him in to the mounting position again. A tough case might require me getting down from my perch on the mounting block to work the horse on the ground. But all along the way, I will be careful to notice where the horse's mind is and be working to get it with me on the task at hand. When that comes together, the task itself gets easier—just one more good feeling spot between me and the horse where the horse can be calm and confident.

Examples in writing like the above help to illustrate my point. Of course, other real world situations may look quite different and present a variety of challenges not covered here specifically. But, regardless of what mounting problems a horse is presenting, the underlying issue of distracted equine thoughts is primary to any improvement. To leave you with another one of my favorite sayings from Harry that is so true and pertinent here: "Until you see it, you can't see it, and when you finally do see it, you wonder how you never saw *that* before!"

I have shared that quote in many of my horsemanship books because I have experienced it myself countless times. But how true. And the realm of mounting, many times a person sees the horse "misbehaving" but hasn't noticed that the horse's mind has left the scene. Point out the horse's distracted mind and when the person sees it and begins to address it, often that is when things finally improve. Consistently keep your focus on where your horse has his focus and you may find that getting that horse happy to stand to be mounted quickly becomes the norm rather than the exception.

The Year Jubal
Saved Christmas

Jubal (The Wonder Horse) in a December snow here in the mountains of Virginia.

Christmas morning arrived. I awoke thinking about the forecast from the night before with its talk of wintry weather. I reached out from under the covers for the flashlight which sat atop the "currently active" pile of books on the nightstand. A small click and there was light, although I was thoughtful to keep some fingers over most of the lens to dampen the brightness.

The sliver of a beam revealed that the clock read 5:57. My wife Carol slept soundly on the other side of her equally zonked Rhodesian Ridgeback/English Mastiff cross dog, Teeney Weeney. Teeney acquired his misnomer due to being the runt of the litter. The name had stuck, even long after he outweighed a yearling heifer. Apparently he'd spent Christmas Eve acquiring territory the size of Montana, Wyoming, and Idaho in the middle of the bed.

I quietly exited my sliver of mattress surface, territory the size of Delaware by comparison to the dog's vast spread—then watched the sorry bugger stretch out and contentedly occupy that space, too. Slipping into a flannel shirt, jeans, socks, and a wool vest, I stepped carefully out of the bedroom, through a sitting room to the stairwell, downstairs, across the great room, outside to the front porch for an armload of firewood, back in, and over to the woodstove. The trip was complicated. Most of our five kids were home that year for Christmas along with a son-in-law and a couple of grandkids. The whole way I had tiptoed past bodies strewn on couches and air mattresses on the floor, and by sleeping dogs in various kennel crates everywhere, upstairs and down. Luckily, nobody had gotten stepped on and no dogs decided I was a dubious character.

I cracked open the woodstove door. The coals lit up. A sizeable bank of charred wood remained from the night before. With a quick stoking it roared to life. The flickering light exposed the white pine Christmas tree reaching to the ceiling not far behind me. I turned briefly to admire it and noticed the mountain of wrapped packages piled underneath. It wouldn't be long now....

The woodstove refueled, I ropewalked between an air mattress and a dog crate and grabbed my outerwear from a rocking chair, pulled on my boots, and quietly slipped through the door into the tack/mud room. Cold air bit my uncovered face and hands. I lifted my thick leather shotgun chaps from where they hung on a saddle horn and smiled thinking that they were stiff enough from the cold to stand up on their own. Zipping them tightly around my legs, I finally headed out the door and peered around at the subtly dawning day.

It was snowing. Apparently flurries were just beginning to fall since the ground did not yet have a dusting.

"What an excellent way to start Christmas!" I thought,

looking up at the myriad flakes whirling around.

I'm a white Christmas kind of guy, although I don't mind reasonable weather for long stretches on either side of that special day. The wintry confetti falling from the sky seemed festive at first. Clouds loomed heavy and low to the ridge tops. Daylight was increasing in a diffused gray glow, but darkness draped the edges of the little clearing on the wooded ridge where our house stands.

"Snow clouds, for sure," I thought. "This is setting in."

With a spring in my step, I headed over to a stash of hay bales in a shed to start feeding horses. Then it happened so quickly…not half way across the yard the snow changed from a flurry of pleasant little flakes to a barrage of more sinister, sharp ice pellets. They began pecking me in the face, stinging like blasts of icy bird shot as the wind whipped them in horizontal waves.

Our little farm is tucked away in the Appalachian Mountains of Virginia. A horseshoe bend of the Little River—aptly named as it is just a stone's throw wide through these parts—acts as one meandering border of the property. The other boundary lines ramble worse than the river. It makes me wonder how people ever concocted some ridiculous series of landmarks to get a piece of land with a plot that looks like an amoeba.

"I'll give you from the old oak at the road, to the quartz rock in the corner of the pasture, to that place where old Kate threw a shoe when we were plowing that time, over to the Hickory there by the spring, then cut over to the river where I got the fishing line stuck in the tree and nearly caught a squirrel that time…" and that's about the only way I can think of that these borders came to be. I could throw a cow pie at a barn side and have fewer wild edges in that splat than this place has.

But for all the creative and bewildering surveying that went into shaping this farm, I am grateful that it is nicely secluded. The river frontage is vast and isolated. The land has two ridges that fall to a central valley running through the middle of the amoeba (if you can imagine an amoeba with a middle). The original home place still stands down there—corrugated metal roof intact, old metal bed frames remain in their bedrooms, ragged clothes from the 1950s are strewn about, and buzzards roost in the upper and lower windows nowadays—and further down the valley a spring shoots out of a hillside from under a huge tree, improved more than a century ago with an alcove of dry laid river rock. Its sparkling clear water still flows from a quartz channel.

When we first moved to this land there was nothing here besides the long abandoned, unlivable house and the spring along with 30 years of unbridled growth, mainly trees and thorny multifloral roses. We cleared a spot on a nice flat ridge with southern exposure for our homestead, a task accomplished with chainsaw and pickup truck, and the help of two Alpine goats, Boudreaux and Sancho. It is a particularly good spot for a homestead the way higher ridges, both on this property and at a distance on others, nearly encircle us breaking up the winds which howl in from North Carolina, Tennessee, West Virginia, and apparently at times the Arctic.

In the early days, I collected the spring and fed the water into a ram pump I built from pipe fittings that delivered water to the home site, some 90 vertical feet up a hill, without any other energy input...no electricity or fuel. It was a pretty cool deal and worked okay for us during the first half decade we lived on the land and build our home and established our gardens, blueberries, and grape vines. We were off-grid with solar power for the first decade living here but eventually brought in grid power, dug a well, and got most of the sheetrock finished. It is this spring way down in a valley far from the house that is the key to how Jubal saved Christmas that year.

Jubal and his bestest buddy, Festus—two big boned, sizable, ranch type American Quarter Horses—had been rescued out of El Paso, Texas earlier in the year. Jubal, a powerful sorrel with ginormous rounded muscles, a long blaze bisecting his face along a Roman nose, and ironically (since I'm Tom Moates) sporting a TM freeze brand on the right hind quarter, had come off a ranch in the Dakotas. Festus, a horse matched to Jubal in height and bone but by the time I first saw him not muscle, was a dark, nearly black, bay with an S Bar Lazy S hot branded on his left hind quarter; he had been a pack guide's horse in Montana. These two had been purchased, paired up, and ridden from Canada to Mexico by a novice horseman from the U.K.

After a long story involving some fancy networking to get the duo here to Virginia, I'd begun working with them. Surprisingly, or perhaps not so surprisingly, both of these very experienced ranch/packing/long ride horses were terrified of ropes. I supposed wrecks involving ropes in the five months they trekked between North Dakota and Texas with an inexperienced rider had plenty to do with that. I'd been working mainly with Jubal since they had arrived because Festus required a long term recovery from a tendon injury he had sustained on that long journey. I'd spent time getting the sorrel gelding more settled around lead ropes and lariats, but at the time I was a complete novice myself when it came to roping.

By the time I had walked only fifty yards to the paddock closest to the house, the icy flurries had intensified. I threw a ration of hay over the fence to a couple geldings, Niji and Stoney. I took time to top out their water trough thinking if this weather knocked out the power later in the day I'd best have as much water stored up for them as possible.

The sleety snow kept up the quick crescendo as I walked over to the farm road and hopped in the pickup. Such an onslaught of wintry weather in so short a time got me thinking about my preparations in case this holiday wintry mix turned into a full blown blizzard. The gray gravel of the road already had begun to take on a white hue as I drove along it. I stopped at the upper end of the valley mentioned earlier and threw several piles of hay over a fence to a small herd of horses in a paddock there, including Jubal and Festus.

I returned to the pickup and continued to the furthest outpost of the property—a pasture near the entrance to the place with a roomy run-in shed that is home to Carol's solitary and flashy Paint stallion, Chief. With his hay placed in the shed and water checked, I descended back into the valley and up the other side, the truck tires now cutting small tracks in the sleet and snow.

It being Christmas, before long the bustle of that special morning was underway. The kitchen, dining, and main living space in our house are all combined into one great room, and with everybody's beds rolled up, this space was getting a big workout. The tree's white lights twinkled like stars and it had some ornaments up high out of reach of the dogs. Homemade buttermilk biscuits came out of the oven and the smell of smoked bacon permeated everything. We have a huge table, and it proved barely large enough to accommodate the crew that morning. Everyone ate, breakfast was cleared, and the kitchen stayed busy with preparations for the afternoon feast. The winds were gusting steadily now, and the and ice estimates kept ticking upwards every time I checked the weather.

The timing was uncanny…just four hours after I'd awoken, we gathered to open presents and as the first one was being picked from under the tree, the tree went dark. The power was out. In these mountains back in hollers where only a few families live on farms, suffice it to say we're not the main concern of the power company. One of the unique attributes of this place is that the only way in is a road cut into a hillside, about one and a half cars wide which I affectionately call "the gauntlet." For a quarter mile it runs along an open ridge with hay fields on either side. With as little as four inches of snow, I've seen this road drift eight feet deep and we've been stranded back in here for more than a week before the state borrowed a snow blowing machine that looked like a combine to literally eat through the snow drift and throw it out across the fields.

We got oil lamps and candles lit, opened presents, and the talk quickly turned to matters regarding the situation. Carol was perturbed because the Christmas day parade couldn't be viewed, but otherwise she had the kids home and was content. The other adults began to think about being stranded in this wilderness and not making their scheduled departures and returns to work. As for me, I don't mind a little bit of winter, or a white Christmas.

In fact, there is something cathartic about having the normal situations of life turned onto their heads. We go about everyday with light switches working and computers always at

Harry used Jubal as a saddle horse for his run of clinics at Mendin' Fences Farm in Rogersville, Tennessee one year. I snapped this shot showing that Jubal wasn't feeling to bad about the rope by this point.

the ready and we expect them to be there always as natural elements of our lives, like the air we breath. Traveling about at will with our cars and planes is the same deal, but when something happens and the grid goes down or the roads become impassible or a volcano shuts down air travel, human constructed comforts suddenly can seem fragile and pretty puny in the big picture.

In these moments we glimpse the greatness of the world

around us and how small and powerless we truly are. I take some delight in the fact that we honestly control but little, and I enjoy being reminded of how foolish and grandiose we humans often are. There is something very settling to me when I'm faced with an overwhelming reality—little things like not being able to find a wrench I need or my e-mail program automatically updating to look nothing like it used to can cause me extreme distress, but life's blizzards just calm me right down and I find a strange solace to them. There is an acceptance in the overwhelmingness of them that comes over me, and then I go about doing what little things I can do to help in such circumstances.

"God's voice is glorious in the thunder," the Bible says in Job 37. "We can't even imagine the greatness of His power. He directs the snow to fall on the earth and tells the rain to pour down. Then everyone stops working so they can watch His power."

The sleet turned back to snow and fell so hard the tree line some 50 yards from the house wasn't visible at moments. Another reason Carol and I don't worry too much about this sort of thing is that we are always pretty prepared for trouble around here. We expect it, and the lifestyle accommodates it. We grow and can much of our own food, so in December, the pantry is plenty full with colorful jars. We have potatoes and sweet potatoes stored up by the bushel. There was plenty of hay on hand that year. We heat the house with wood and cook with propane, so our inconvenience was limited.

On top of all that, we have solar power. For a decade we were totally off-grid, but by the time this Christmas came around, we had brought in grid power but retained our solar panels and deep cycle batteries. The problem was that lightning had taken out our inverter the summer before and we had not yet been able to replace it. This left us with no backup power, and the big problem when that happens is that we can't run the well pump. We had a pretty good store of drinking water in plastic bottles in the pantry, so we wouldn't die from thirst even if we were stranded for days. But we had a house full of people, and that means a lot of dirty dishes and more than a few flushes.

Everything went smoothly with the food fixins, and other than the sadly unilluminated Christmas tree, we had fun watching the snow, playing cards, and just catching up on life. After the mid-afternoon main Christmas dinner, the true trouble began to show. Dirty pans and dishes were piled everywhere. We all caught ourselves habitually turning faucet handles and flipping light switches even though we knew better.

The roads by this time were really bad. With the wind and cold snowy forecast, the drifts would continue to pile up and re-cover the roads that did get plowed. There wasn't even a hope of folks leaving or the power coming back on for a couple of days. Something had to be done to get some water to the house or, with a crew this big, our good holiday cheer shortly would start to suffer severely.

I thought about melting snow in a pot or two on the wood stove, but if you've ever tried that task you know it takes about ten feet of snow to get a cup of water—that would never cover even a handful of flushes in a day. No, we needed something much more bold. I remembered the spring down in the valley. Carrying water uphill that distance in this weather wouldn't be much better than melting snow. We didn't have a tractor at the time and there was no way to get the truck back out if I drove down there. Hmm…but then it occurred to me, I had Jubal (The Wonder Horse)! That burly beast could easily lug both me and a ton of water up out of the valley. I got my plan together.

I got a rope halter and fetched Jubal out of the paddock in the bottom and led him up to the house to the tack room. A layer of ice and snow covered his back which I curried off the best I could and tacked him up in a western saddle and bridle with rope mecate reins. That was the easy part. My plan was to get a bunch of gallon jugs (luckily Carol had been saving them all summer to use as mini tomato green houses in the spring), run my rope through the handles, and then take a dally and have Jubal drag the lot of them over the icy snow. Great plan, but

Jubal (The Wonder Horse) is in the middle between Niji, to the left, and Festus, who is looking at something that has caught his interest. They are enjoying hay in the valley pasture where they were staying during the Christmas power outage.

there was the issue of Jubal's fear about ropes. And, I wondered how plastic jugs scootching along the gritty snow would add to his concern, especially being behind him.

I gathered a school of jugs and threaded the handles onto a long rope. These I dragged along behind me while I led Jubal a short distance across the yard. He was uncertain at first and danced around anytime the plastic jugs moved on the icy ground. The heavy raining of ice pellets and wind combined to make a constant roar around us, not helping to ease Jubal's mind. My boots and Jubal's unshod feet crunched through several inches of the snow/sleet mix with each step.

As I dragged the empty jugs and walked along side the big gelding I would move the rope closer to his side and towards the saddle horn. When he showed apprehension, I'd hang in there until he'd give at least a hint of relaxation about it and then I'd take the rope away and pet on him. We repeated this process over and over and he got better and better about the rope and the load behind him. The worst part was that the saddle was starting to look like the road with an opaque white icy frosting, which I knew was going to be a bum freezer when I got aboard.

Finally, I was able to reach over and take a dally on the saddle horn and for about the last half of the trip down to the spring, Jubal pulled the empty jugs himself as I led him from the side.

A short PVC pipe stuck out of the dam and clear spring water poured out in a constant stream. I held the lead rope from the mecate, not wanting to risk tying Jubal to a tree as he was getting very jittery being away from his buddies and in a strange situation, and multitasked filling the jugs. I'd brought 15 or 20. It took awhile to get the lot of them topped out, capped, and then restrung on the rope while trying to keep a jittery Jubal focused and steady. Finally, I had them all set. I tested the load and it was a heavy pull, even over the inches of sleety snow on the ground. My hands were freezing and I stuck them under Jubal's thin mane until the stabbing pain subsided.

I turned Jubal to face the direction we needed to head for home and backed him up to the load. I cleared the saddle of ice the best I could, took a handful of rein and mane in one hand, had the water jug rope and cantle in the other, put a foot in the stirrup, and pulled myself up.

When Jubal first came to me he was terrible about walking off when I'd go to mount. I'd worked a bunch on getting his mind centered with me in general, and when I was successful with that, as a pleasant by-product, when going to mount, he'd stand fine. He wasn't the best this time…the situation was big for him considering the adverse conditions, and I wasn't handy enough to get him really mentally with me in such a spot. Not to mention I was anxious to see how it would go. With the trees whipping wildly all through the valley, Jubal stepped ahead the second I got my leg across him.

Luckily, he backed when I asked him to with the reins, but he stayed put only a second before piaffing to charge ahead. I backed him again, took a dally, and tried to ease him forward. I could feel the weight of the water stretch the rope tight as I floated Jubal some slack on the reins. The muscular Quarter Horse shot forward, the cloud of white jugs slid along the sleet behind us, and off we went!

Once moving, things smoothed out. The first leg of the trip proved super easy because the gelding wanted to return to his buddies and a pile of hay which were on the way to the house. Once there, it took some urging from the saddle to put that in his rear view mirror, but I managed.

We arrived in the yard by the house with our precious load of water. A few jugs had busted and drained along the way, but at least three-quarters of them made the journey intact. I dropped my dally, dismounted, untacked Jubal, and then got The Wonder Horse turned out again with Festus and the others, and his hay. I returned to the house and began hauling the jugs inside; the relief of the humans was palpable. We flushed and washed dishes, and getting the place cleaned up made a huge improvement in moral.

The story didn't end there…it was two days before the kids got out, and two more before we had power again, but Jubal and I made more water runs. And by providing this present to us, Jubal really did save Christmas that year. When I reflect on this fairly simple, yet enormously helpful, role a horse played in my life, my mind wanders further and considers how horses really have helped shape humanity's modernity and how much we have to thank them for.

The horse was the very first means by which we were able to travel overland beyond the speed of our own flat feet. The horse altered our sense of time when for the first time a letter

Jubal has improved his abilities to relax and keep his mind with me in many situations as displayed in this photo that I like to call "just another day at the office." (Photo: Carol Moates)

could outpace a pedestrian when carried by a rider or wagon, and goods could be moved around en mass. Still today in remote country that cannot be accessed by trucks, four wheelers, or motorcycles, horses make it possible to open up the land for ranching and managing cattle and other stock to produce food and goods for people. The list goes on and on.

So with another Christmas close at hand I think back

and say thanks, Jubal, to you and all of your equine kind for tolerating us humans and helping us out over the centuries. I only hope we return the favor.... And Merry Christmas!

About the Author

Tom Moates is a leading equestrian author and journalist. This award winning writer is on the masthead of *Equus* magazine as a Contributing Writer, and his articles have run in many horse magazines in the United States and abroad including: *Eclectic Horseman*, *America's Horse*, and *Western Horseman*. Moates's previous books include the *Six Colts, Two Weeks* trilogy, and his other titles, *Discovering Natural Horsemanship*, *A Horse's Thought*, *Between the Reins*, *Further Along the Trail*, *Going Somewhere*, *Passing It On*, and *Round-Up: A Gathering of Equine Writings*. Recently Moates took a foray into fiction and published *The Old Sleeper*, a spy novel— and yes, it does have horses in it! Moates lives on a solar powered farm with his wife Carol and a herd of horses in the Blue Ridge Mountains of Virginia. Book ordering info, horsemanship clinic and lesson info, and Moates's latest publishing news are available at www.TomMoates.com.

Mirage, Miles (my neighbor's mini-poodle), and me with Jubal and Festus in the background wishing all y'all the best in your horsemanship endeavors—have fun! (Photo: Teddy Carter)

CPSIA information can be obtained
at www.ICGtesting.com
Printed in the USA
BVHW052231300922
648456BV00004B/60